S0-EGI-161

PLUMP

SURVIVAL OF THE FATTEST

To Linda –
Hope you enjoy this.
It's great having you
next door!
Best wishes!
Linda F. Carlson

written & illustrated by

Linda Frantzen Carlson

edited by

Laurie Boucke

LAFAYETTE, COLORADO

First Published October 1999

ISBN 1-888580-12-7

Printed in the United States of America

Library of Congress Cataloging-in-Publication Data

Carlson, Linda (Linda Frantzen), 1949-
Plump : survival of the fattest / written & illustrated by Linda Frantzen Carlson ; edited by Laurie Boucke.
p. cm.
ISBN 1-888580-12-7
1. Carlson, Linda (Linda Frantzen), 1949---Health. 2. Overweight women--United States Biography. 3. Weight loss Humor. I. Boucke, Laurie. II. Title.
RC628.C378 1999
362.1'96398'0092--dc21
[B] 99-43574
CIP

www.white-boucke.com

Dedicated to
Ronald McDonald, Chiquita Banana,
and Mama Celeste

Cooperatively illustrated by
Linda, Tessa, and Traci Carlson

Contents

PROLARD

You Know Your Preoccupation with Food Has Become a Sickness When...

- You're picked up by a policeman, thrown in jail, and you waste your one phone call by dialing Mario's Pizzeria to order a 22-inch Special Deluxe with everything on it except anchovies. (There are, after all, some foods even *you* won't eat.)
- You unwittingly eat in your sleep and wake up with a chocolate bar stuck to your face.
- You walk in your sleep and wake up to find yourself in the kitchen making brownies.
- The way you measure your character is quite simple, really: You're "good" if you don't eat, and "bad" if you do.
- You offer to run to McDonalds to pick up lunch for the family. You order an extra extra value meal and wolf it down in the car on your way home. You then eat the regular order with your family, all the while making a big issue of how full that silly little burger and fries are making you.
- You go to your kitchen for a paper towel or some such nonedible item and suddenly find

yourself staring glassy-eyed into the belly of your opened refrigerator.

- You eat when you're sad, happy, lonely, depressed, afraid, secure, embarrassed, proud, mad, anxious, calm, ad nauseam. But eating out of hunger has become just a shadowy childhood memory.

- You spend a lot of time picking out diets you'll start tomorrow and drawing up expected weight-loss graphs, eating all the while, because it's imperative that you go on one last binge. (The weight-loss graphs, incidentally, never contain more than one follow-up entry.)

- Your rationale begins to falter, and you begin to say things like, "If drinking one diet milkshake for lunch will help me lose weight, surely drinking two will do the trick twice as fast."

- You decide against buying those desperately needed new clothes, rationalizing that it would be a waste of money, because, considering the overwhelming success of those new combination diet pills you've been reading about, in less than a month the clothes would be far too big for you anyway. You buy a box of Ho Hos to celebrate and eat them all in one sitting.

- Your psychiatrist tells you you really need to lighten up, and you immediately stick your finger down your throat.

- You eat everything as though you're practicing for the county fair's pie-eating contest, and when the food's gone you wonder what it tasted like.
- You become a closet eater (and a car eater).
- You eat to avoid hurting someone's feelings.
- You have a hard time remembering whether today it's calories that count, or fat, or carbohydrates, or protein, or fiber, or all of them, or none of them . . .
- You're convinced that as soon as you've suffered through an agonizing diet and get down to your "ideal" (whatever that is) weight, someone will come up with a miracle drug that causes the fat to just melt off, so you prefer to wait.
- You secretly wish you had a tapeworm.
- Other people are asked if they'd care for an appetizer. You're simply handed a plate.
- You salivate when your computer screen prompts you to make a selection from the menu.
- You wear a disguise at all-you-can-eat restaurants.
- You sneak candy from your children's Halloween bags when they're not at home. (In order to be fair, you take exactly the same number of pieces from each of their bags.)

- One friend says her weakness is bread, another admits his is chocolate, still another says hers is ice cream, and you simply nod in agreement.

* * * * *

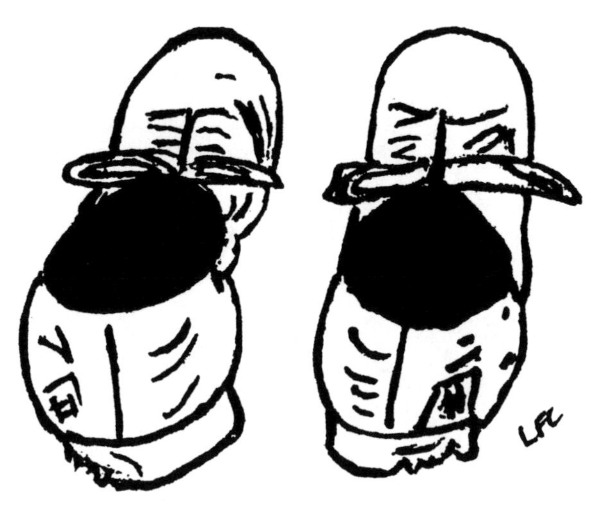

1

What's So Pleasant About Plump?

August 23, 1962—Today is my thirteenth birthday. A teenager at last! I went to cheerleader tryouts this afternoon. They didn't pick me. When I tried to do a cartwheel, Mary Sue Miller laughed and said, "Don't you know you're too fat to be a cheerleader?"

"I think that I shall never see" . . .
a person quite as fat as me.

I don't know about you, but I'm sick to death of hearing compliments like, "You're light on your feet . . . for a fat person," "You've got such a great personality" (read fat people really are jolly), and "You're not exactly *fat,* just pleasantly plump." I've personally never found much pleasure in anything plump, with the possible exception of sunbathing next to someone plumper than me.

You're out on a date (blind, of course), and the nicest thing the fellow can think of to say to you is, "You don't sweat much for a fat girl." A friend reminisces about the past, quipping, "I remember you could keep a hula hoop up longer than anyone on the block, and all you had to do was step into it!" Your brother describes a girl he's just met saying, "She was even fatter than you!" Your sister says, "This shirt is way too big for me. Maybe you could wear it." You've struggled for months to get down to what you consider a decent weight, and your boyfriend says, "Don't give up now, you're almost there!" Your preteen spies you naked and later with obvious trepidation whispers, “Mommy, will *I* be fat when I grow up?” A stranger approaches you in a mall and, with a knowing smile, asks, “Due in a couple of months?” How do you deal with the inevitable embarrassment, anxiety, and depression that follows one of these episodes?

I go somewhere and eat. Stuff my lardy lips until my jaws cramp up from overexertion.

*****

Kids are great too. “Someday I’ll be as fat as you.” “You’re squishy.” “Hey! Don’t sit on my chair, you’ll break it!” Cute little dumplin’s. A part of you would like to rip out their tongues or perhaps beat them with one of their scrawny little legs.

But despite all their verbalized innuendoes, the worst one, the most cutting, belittling, embarrassing one is without words. It’s when you’ve agreed to play run through the sprinkler on a hot summer day with them, and you merrily don your “flaw-concealing” swimsuit and dash back out into the yard to play. At once *a silence comes over the world. All movements come to a sudden halt.* Then those little creatures with whom you found it in the goodness of your heart to play, slowly face each other, eyes sparkling. They cup their pukey, grimy little hands over their mouths and *giggle!* Aaarggh! You feel hideous and realize for the first time that no matter how fat you may have believed your adipose-altered upper appendages to be, they’re just not large enough to conceal your entire, enormous entity. Suddenly you’re struck with the dilemma that has befallen you. You must either stay and endure their ridicule, or turn quickly and run away, and by so doing, allow them to see (and no doubt point at) your bountiful, bouncing backside. Oh, that this too, too, sufficient flesh would melt.

*****

You're self-consciously strolling down the street, testing mind-over-matter techniques, unsuccessfully willing your fat not to jiggle while you walk. From a distance you hear a wolf whistle. How do you react? In a crowd, I generally don't react, assuming the whistle wasn't intended for me. If, on the other hand, I'm alone on the street, I am mortified by the whistle, convinced I'm the butt of some cruel joke. Driven by humiliation, I dash with Wonder Woman-like speed around the nearest corner, acutely aware that, unlike my stomach, neither my hips nor my thighs are equipped with an automatic suck-in option.

If you're the least bit rotund, you've probably noticed that your personal belongings take on certain characteristics that enable you to recognize them as yours without having to go through the traditional trouble of sewing on name tags. For example . . .

- After a month's wear, the heels of your shoes are worn down (or off) on the outer sides.
- Your blue jeans are worn through, not on the seat and knees as is the current fashion, but on the *inside of the thighs.*
- The inner thighs of all your sweat pants have seen so much friction that they've deteriorated into a mass of little cloth balls that dangle between your legs.

- Your bookshelf looks as though it has been plucked from the waiting room of a weight-loss clinic.
- You can easily recognize your car in a crowded parking lot, because the driver's side sits much closer to the ground than the passenger's side.
- The main staples of your wardrobe are sweat suits, smocks, and overblouses—if it's form-fitting, it must belong to someone else.

Recognize anything so far? If so, I've probably seen you at a magazine rack somewhere, furtively searching through the tables of contents for the latest "miracle." If not, don't stop here. Reading this little book may be the closest you'll ever get to a true fat experience!

* * * * *

2

One Potato,
Two Potato,
Three Potato, Four ...

January 30, 1965—Penney's had a presummer special on swimming suits today. I bought a baby blue one that's way too small. I've got five months until June. If I start tomorrow, I should be able to lose sixty pounds by summer.

I once worked with a woman who said that during her entire childhood, in an attempt to get her and her sisters to clean their plates, her mother would always use the timeworn, guilt-provoking line, "Think of all the children in China who are starving."

My coworker said that every time her mother made that comment, she couldn't help wondering how her cleaning her plate would in any way benefit even one starving child on the other side of the world, and she pointed out the apparent irrationality to her mother. But, to no avail. Her mother continued to chant the line for years, at just about every meal. Eventually tired of hearing the line, by this time a teenager, my coworker thought of something she hoped would make her mother back off. The next time her mother said "Think of all the children in China who are starving," my friend looked her straight in the eye and challenged, "Yeah? Name *one!*"

We've all heard the rationalization that if you're fat today, you can blame it on your mother. In my particular case, I can't agree. My mom never said things like, "Waste not, want not," and, "Think of all the children in China who are starving," to make us feel guilty enough to eat. She never had to. The fact is, that poor lady went through pains to *hide* food from her kids. But we were relentless in our searches and always persevered until we found whatever it was she had hidden, threats to life and limb notwithstanding.

Wounds were incurred as we leaped off of the kitchen counters at the sound of her voice. "What are you kids doing in there?" We would glance at each other, smother a giggle, and shout through the closed kitchen door, "Nothing, Mom!"

But, like most mothers, ours always had this sort of ESP when it came to her kids. She knew that *nothing* was our secret code word for *something* and always managed to allow us just enough time to resume our strategic positions, heads and arms deep within the belly of the cupboards, searching frantically for the chocolate chips we knew just had to be there somewhere, when soundlessly, she would appear at the door behind us. "*What* are you kids looking for?"

Cracking my head on the upper shelf, I would make a meager attempt to remove myself from the cupboard and pretend, illuminated flashlight in hand, that she had simply been hallucinating. Sheepishly, I would whisper, "Oh, nothing."

But she always knew exactly what it was we were looking for. "Well, the chocolate chips aren't in there. Now, get down from that counter before you hurt yourselves."

As I said, we were relentless in our search. Upon spotting the brown and yellow bag that contained the tiny chocolate morsels, one of us would gingerly grasp the bag by a corner with thumb and forefinger, so as to avoid the telltale crackle of cellophane, while the other feigned a coughing spell designed to camouflage any wayward sounds of sneaking. We would then scurry to that corner of the house farthest from Mom's sensitive ears, and there in the darkness, we'd scarf down the entire bag of little chocolate pieces. Mission accomplished, we would then tiptoe to one of our rooms and do something noisy to make sure Mom knew where we were (definitely not the kitchen) and have no reason to become suspicious.

Our secret remained sacred until Mom got the urge to make cookies. *Cookies.* The word spelled doom, and sneaking off to hide in my room, I hoped that the storm would somehow pass in my absence. It never did. Mom would appear at my bedroom door, looking knowingly at the part in the top of my head, as I did my best to look engrossed in the Hardy Boys. "Where are the chocolate chips?" she would ask through gritted teeth.

I would slowly raise my head, eyes scanning the room for the empty bag, and say in the closest thing to cherub-speak I could manage, "What chocolate chips?"

Shaking her head, she would sigh wearily and leave for the grocery store.

Immediately I would suffer unbearable guilt. What if she had an accident? She only went to the store because *I* had helped eat the chocolate chips! I would sit at the kitchen window, biting my nails until I saw her car pulling back into the driveway. Then, to make penance for my sin, I would run down to meet her and offer to help carry in the groceries and bake the cookies. (Although, admittedly, this wasn't *too* great a sacrifice . . . Mom always let me eat some of the dough.)

No, it definitely wasn't my mother's fault. However, it was, in my opinion, at least partially the fault of a mother with whom we are all too familiar. Good ol' Mother Goose. I have a misery-loves-company theory concerning her. It is my guess that Mother Goose was the first to be stricken with a weight problem, and her rhymes were maliciously created, not to soothe the children of the world, as is commonly believed, but to plant visions of sugar plums in fertile little minds, which would eventually evolve into the uncontrollable desire for food that plagued *her.* Just take a look at a few of the many seeds she planted. . .

Jack Sprat could eat no fat,
His wife could eat no lean . . .

Pat-a-cake, pat-a-cake, baker's man!
Make me a cake as fast as you can . . .

Georgie Porgie, puddin' and pie . . .

Sing a song of sixpence,
A pocket full of rye;
Four and twenty blackbirds
Baked in a pie . . .

To market, to market,
To buy a plum cake . . .

Peas Porridge hot,
Peas porridge cold . . .

Little Miss Muffett,
Sat on a tuffet,
Eating her curds and whey . . .

Peter Piper picked a peck of pickled peppers . . .

Polly put the kettle on . . .

The queen of hearts,
She made some tarts . . .

Simple Simon met a pieman . . .

Oh, did you see the muffin man,
The muffin man, the muffin man? . . .

Little Jack Horner
Sat in a corner,
Eating a Christmas pie;
He put in his thumb,
And pulled out a plum,
And said, 'What a good boy am I'

Sugar and spice,
And everything nice . . .

Hot cross buns!
Hot cross buns! . . .

The list goes on and on, chanting about cakes and sweets and dishes and spoons. Even if no malice was intended, I can't help but believe that some harm may have been done by the food fixation apparent in these familiar little ditties.

Whatever the cause, my romance with food began in early childhood. I was both fickle and jealous when it came to my love. I enjoyed all the sweet, sticky things that were supposed to rot your teeth, and I was an unusual child in that I also became euphoric over foods that the other kids said made them want to puke. I was in heaven while eating my second helping of liver and onions; delirious at the sight of a steaming dish of creamed spinach. In fact, I ate almost anything I could get my chubby little hands on. I even used to eat one *Milk Bone* dog biscuit for every two I gave the dog.

Observing the cattle on my grandparent's farm opened up a whole new category of edibles for me that would have shocked even Euell Gibbons's liberal taste buds. I remember watching jealously as the cows slurped at the salt lick or chomped lazily at the grass in the fields. I tried both and found I really enjoyed being on all fours eating sweet clover with "Old Boss." And when I was sure Grandpa wasn't looking, I would dip my fingers into the cows' pail of blackstrap molasses and have myself a little taste.

In first grade, I discovered a way to curb those annoying hunger pangs that always appeared as the afternoons dragged on. I'd wager that over the grade school years, I consumed at least one ream of lined writing paper. But, my favorite schooltime staple was paste. I'm sure you know the kind I'm talking about. It came in a little cylindrical jar that had an orange lid with a brush attached to it. Well, I can attest to the fact that that paste not only smelled like peppermint, it tasted like it too.

Now, on the other hand, tapioca pudding was an entirely different matter. It was the one thing I wouldn't eat, and only because of a rather tasteless trick my father played on me the first time I ever laid eyes on the stuff. I was just about to dip my spoon into my dessert when I first noticed them—the bumps. Using my spoon to turn one over for a closer look, I innocently asked, "Daddy, what are those little lumps in this pudding?"

His face didn't give the slightest hint that he was anything but sincere as he answered, "Frog eyes."

Well, really! Even I, self-appointed junior cosmopolite of the food world, couldn't go that far! I still have a vague recollection of Dad's eyes sparkling as he polished off both of our desserts that night.

*****

Outwardly, mine was a fairly normal childhood. Like all the other girls I knew, I graduated from Brownie (love that name!) to Girl Scout, not through any real effort of my own, but simply because I had attained a certain age. I stuck it out because my mom always bought and froze every box of cookies I had to sell. (I convinced her early on that I wasn't cut out for a career in sales.)

I attended Girl Scout camp, where I learned to do all the usual Girl Scout things, like staying in cabins, sleeping in bunkbeds, and telling ghost stories at night, holding a lighted flashlight under my double chin to create a special effect. Judging from the other girls' reactions, it must have been a pretty scary sight.

We learned to burn campfire stew so it stuck to the bottom of a Folger's coffee can, and we drank water out of canteens and learned to smother our campfires with dirt. But, truth be known, the one and only thing I learned in Girl Scout camp that I still carry with me today, is how to make s'mores out of graham crackers, marshmallows, and melted Hershey bars . . .

On sunny days, we kids played outdoor games that had sweet little names like "Double Dutch" and "Hopscotch." And on those days it chanced to rain, we would play inside-games like Go Fish, Candyland, or Waffle Blocks. If we got tired of those, we'd make something with our Easy Bake Ovens, or read about Cinderella, who had a coach made out of a pumpkin, of all things!

I was soon to discover that fat was something that made you stand apart. Something that people liked to laugh at. In my *salad* days, before I knew better, I used to sing chants like, "Fatty, fatty, two-by-four, can't get through the kitchen door." Until I realized we were singing about me. I remember trying to ignore the other kids' giggles as my weak little arms collapsed under the weight of my torso while I clumsily tried to perfect a cartwheel. I was always the last chosen for games requiring speed and agility like tag, but the first chosen to help form the base of a pyramid. I quit ballet after just a couple of lessons. The mirrored walls made it painfully clear to me that if everyone else was wearing a tutu, then mine was obviously a four-four, or if I squinted hard enough, just possibly a three-three.

In high school, all the kids I ran around with had fun nicknames, like Cricket, Froggy, Huey, Hemorrhoid, and Itty Bitty. Depending on who you asked, mine alternated between Chesty, Blubber Butt, and Hippo Hips.

I remember with mortifying clarity the struggle I used to go through to put on a pair of newly washed blue jeans. I would actually work myself into a sweat stuffing my legs into the two narrow openings called pant legs. The next step was a repetition of about twelve deep knee bends, coordinated with fierce upward tugs on the belt loops (one or two of which would invariably be ripped loose from the waistband). This exercise served to slowly inch the crotch of the pants up from between my knees, nearer to its namesake position. This endeavor was of necessity followed by a brief time-out to muster the strength required for the next steps. Once rested, I would stand up, suck in my gut 'til my eyes bulged, and fasten the snap at the waistband. This particular step usually had to be repeated several times, because as I let out my breath, my stomach inevitably came along with it, causing a reaction in the dinky copper snap similar to one I would imagine would occur if a tidal wave were to hit the dike at the precise moment the Little Dutch Boy decided he simply had to pick his nose.

The final step, zipping up the pants, was the most hazardous. I would grasp the tiny metal tongue between my thumb and forefinger and yank skyward, yelping as the teeth of the zipper bit a meaty chunk out of my protruding belly. The zipper resisted, sliding down again and again, and I tugged and tugged until my fingers had been rubbed raw. Defeated, I would put out a call for help.

Lying flat on my back across the bed, I would garner the strength required to once again pull in my stomach as far as was humanly possible, while my mother, gritting her teeth, managed to overpower the uncooperative zipper with the aid of a sturdy pair of Craftsman pliers. (This scene was necessitated by the fact that I had developed a psychological block about buying pants *the next size larger.)*

The battle was won, but certainly not the war. By this time I was so tightly squeezed into the pants that bending my legs had become an impossibility. So, I was forced to rock back and forth on the mattress until I built up enough momentum to thrust my body up from the bed and into a standing position. Once on my feet, I remained that way for hours rather than exert the energy I knew it would take to sit and then get up again. (A sideline benefit of this experience was that I developed a superhuman ability to hold my urine, which I've found can come in really handy on those long road trips when traveling with an insensitive driver.)

It was following one of these little skirmishes that, at the tender age of twelve, I began my lifetime pursuit of the "perfect diet."

* * * * *

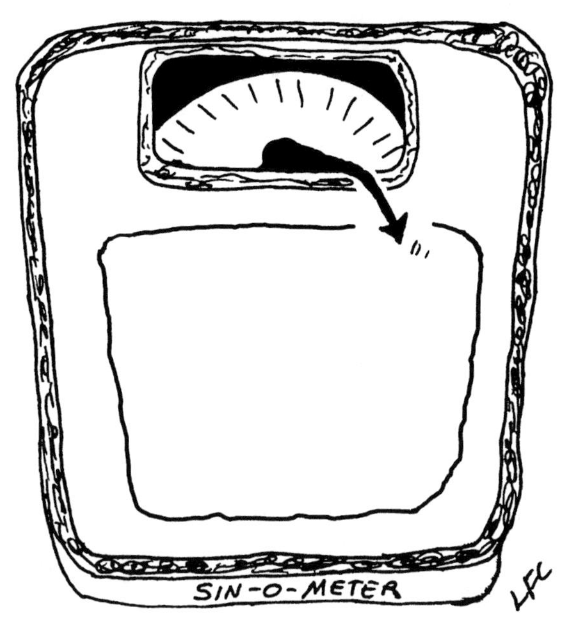

3

The Fat of the Land: Sneak Previews

__May 14, 1966__—Johnny gave me back my ring today. He said he always liked me, but always wished I dressed a little more like Nancy H. He said he also always wished I could be a little more her size. I doubt if I'll ever fill her shoes, let alone fit into her shorts!

Those of us who have a problem with our weight seem to have developed some very creative ways to sneak food. I haven't decided yet if we do it because we're embarrassed to have people watch us eat, afraid they'd be wondering how a person our size could possibly be hungry, or if somewhere deep down inside we truly believe that if no one ever sees us eat, they'll feel sorry for us, assuming we must have this terrible, inexplicable disorder. It has to be something like that. How else do you explain the number of large people at restaurants ordering just a salad with dressing on the side and a diet soda?

I have a friend who vacationed in France and found she just couldn't resist all those gooey pastries the country had to offer. Realizing she would be embarrassed if she actually ordered everything she wanted from one bakery, she found herself traveling from bakery to bakery ordering just one delectable goody from each place. These she would smuggle back to the privacy of her hotel room and eat in one sitting. Then to compensate, she would go out and take a ten-mile bike ride.

*****

In the fall of 1975 I went to San Francisco with some friends. I had been on some diet or other for the two months preceding the trip and had accomplished a modest weight loss, so I wanted to continue with the diet, vacation or not. I was "good" until I got my first whiff of sourdough bread. Then I knew it was a lost cause.

That night at supper on the Wharf, while my friends were in the ladies room, I surreptitiously stuffed the bread we hadn't finished at supper and a handful of individually wrapped butter pats into my purse. Back at the hotel, I waited impatiently for my friends to go to sleep, and when they finally did, sometime in the wee hours of the night, I sat on the bed, in the dark, spreading the softened butter with my index finger and devouring what remained of the sourdough. Unlike the scenario with my friend in France, the thought of riding a bike for ten miles never entered my mind.

*****

I have another friend who used to love popcorn drizzled with butter, but didn't like the sidelong glances she'd get from her husband if she ate it in front of him. So, to avoid his belittling stares at her stomach, two hours before he got home each night, she would defiantly pop herself up a double batch of popcorn, dump half a stick of melted butter over it, sprinkle it with salt, and gobble up the entire bowlful. Afterward, she would clean up all of the evidence—the pans, bowl, and any stray pieces of corn that may have found their way to the floor in her haste to eat the stuff—and take pains to ensure that each item was returned to its original spot in the cupboard. As a final precaution, she would open all the windows (no matter that it was the dead of winter) to get rid of that telltale smell.

Today this same friend adds lard to fat-free refried beans, puts butter on lite popcorn, and drops marshmallows into mugs of sugar-free cocoa. The only rationale I can think of for her seemingly bizarre behavior is that she wants the garbage collectors to notice her empty diet food containers and give her credit for at least trying.

*****

Another friend of mine was one of eleven siblings. Her mother loved bananas, but with a brood that big found that when she brought the bananas home and put them out on the cupboard, they'd be gone before she'd finished bringing in the rest of the groceries. So she used to buy two bunches of bananas and put one on the cupboard for her scavenger children to fight over and hide one in the back of her underwear drawer. Problem was sometimes she got so busy taking care of that many kids, she'd forget about her hidden stash until the smell of overripe bananas brought her running.

*****

I love Butterfinger Chips to the point of becoming aggressive if anyone tries to help themselves to a piece of candy from my box, or even has the nerve to ask me to share. To avoid putting myself in the situation where I would undoubtedly get ticked off or have a roommate think I was not just fat, but fat *and* selfish, one summer I thought I found a solution to a sticky situation. I decided I would only eat the candy in the privacy of my own car. After all, people really can't see you stuffing your face behind that tinted windshield, can they?

Depending on how far away from home I was when I bought the candy, I could eat anywhere from half a box to the entire thing driving home from the grocery store. One especially hot summer afternoon, I bought a box of the candy at a store, which, as it turned out, was far too close to home. I only managed to eat about a quarter of the box before I got home, so ended up hiding what was left in the glove compartment of my car.

The next day I returned to the car and opened the glove compartment, mouth watering for a chocolate-coated, peanut-buttery morsel. I thrust my hand into the glove compartment, pulled out the box, glanced around to make sure no one was watching me, and stuck my hand into a gooey, melted mess of chocolate and butter chip. It seems my attempt to avoid one sticky situation had just put me in the middle of a stickier one.

*****

A good friend of mine had volunteered to host a get-together for our fifteen-year high school reunion. In high school she had been unceremoniously dumped for someone thinner by a guy I considered a really insensitive slob, but one she had been blindly in love with nonetheless. She had always wanted some sort of revenge on this guy. You know, the kind where you have become a thin, beautiful, rich, and famous personality, and the poor sucker is watching you being interviewed one night on *The Tonight Show,* wanting you desperately and kicking himself for ever having let you go.

Well, time for the reunion was drawing nearer and nearer, and my friend still hadn't been invited to appear on *The Tonight Show.* For that matter, she hadn't become thin or rich and famous either (I guess no one ever really thought she had a problem in the beauty department, in fact, you always heard people say the same thing about her: "But she has such a *pretty* face.").

She didn't know if her ex-dumper would be at the reunion, but just on the off chance, she wanted to look as good as she could. (I secretly hoped he'd show up sporting a poorly matched rug, varicose veins, and a beer gut.) So she went on the low-carbohydrate diet that was the then current rage, eating way too many hard-boiled eggs and grapefruit for anyone's good. Over a three-week period of ***really sticking to her diet,*** she miraculously managed to shed about twelve pounds, but felt dizzy most of the time and had nightmares about menacing hot fudge sundaes.

The morning of the party, she bought herself a new black dress (not a *little* black dress, a large black dress; black, of course, because black is touted as having this elusive quality known as "slimming"). She spent most of the rest of the day preparing fancy (some not-so-fancy) hors d'oeuvres for the party.

About two hours before the party, she took a shower, slipped into her large black dress, and began to wait for her guests to arrive. The problem was, she started too early. With time on her hands, she began to wonder if *he*'d be there. She looked in the mirror and began to wonder if she looked okay. She started getting nervous. So, she decided she would eat one of each of the hors d'oeuvres she'd made—just one. And she did, and then she carefully rearranged the rest on the plates so it didn't look like any were missing. Who could tell? But darn those hor d'oeuvres sure tasted good after three weeks of near starvation! Maybe *just one more.* No one would ever know, would they?

By the time the doorbell rang, my friend had eaten far more of the hor d'oeuvres than she had intended; in fact, she hardly remembered eating them at all. Quickly she tore open a bag of chips and dumped them into a bowl. She then divided what was left of the hors d'oeuvres between two platters and hid the other two, now-empty, platters behind the trash basket under the sink. She'd see to them later.

Well, the bum never showed up, and somewhere deep inside, I think my friend was glad. Maybe before the next reunion that rich and famous thing would happen to her. Then she would show him, by George.

After the party I hung around to help her clean up the mess. But she begged me not to stay, mumbling something about lately having this overwhelming passion for domesticity. I think she just wanted me to leave so she could pick through the leftovers in peace.

* * * * *

4

Hey, Moonface, Wanna Buy a Diet?

__June 10, 1967__—I'm depressed. Summer's here again, and I'm still a lard. Brother Ron and the gang went to the reservoir to swim. I told them I didn't feel good. I really don't when I look at myself in a bathing suit. Monday will be six weeks from August first. If I could just lose five pounds a week, I could lose thirty pounds by then. Then maybe I could sneak out in the backyard and get a little tan before classes start.

I have this recurring nightmare that an enterprising man with a mustache and greasy hair appears to me from out of a dark corner, looks suspiciously in all directions, and with a swoop of his right arm, presents me with a bulging array of diets and associated gadgets and gimmicks attached to the inside of his black cloak. He steps closer and whispers in my ear, "Such a deal I have for you!"

My heart palpitates with uncontrollable excitement. Finally my search has ended, for somewhere in this conglomeration must surely hide the key that will unlock the wall of fat that has imprisoned me for so long!

With the finesse of a used car salesman, the guy reaches into his cloak, draws out a likely candidate, and says, "Now, this here little number was made just for you . . ."

I interrupt, saying, "No good, I've tried that one."

Undaunted, he quickly discards it and draws out the next, which I reject, saying, "Nope, sorry, gained on that."

Scowling, he pulls out the next item, and before he can open his mouth, I shake my head and say, "Threw my back out twice with that contraption."

The dream continues this way until, exhausted, the scoundrel removes the last scrap of paper from his by-now frayed cloak. With pleading eyes, he looks at me. Voice cracking, he says, "Ah, this is it! Guaranteed to work. The latest craze in . . ." But before he can finish the jerk falls over and dies.

Disgusted by his poor timing and without the least bit of remorse for this dead flimflam man, like a scavenger, I leap shamelessly on his clenched fist to gain the long-awaited secret. But, as happens in all low-budget science fiction dreams, the creep and all his possessions disintegrate before my disbelieving eyes.

It is that illusive quality of the "perfect diet" that causes me to set up camp the first of every month outside the five and dime to wait with bageled breath, until the magazines come in.

When I walk past the magazine section at any grocery store, it's like I can hear tiny voices screaming, "Hey, you! Yeah, you, gullible fat lady. Here's another one!" Someone out there knows that I'll buy anything printed as long as the words *Weight-Loss Breakthrough* appear somewhere on the front cover. Fortunately for stockholders in the diet industry (which, by the way, currently generates $33 billion in revenues annually!), I'm not the only one.

I'm sure almost everyone can admit to having been duped at least once in their life by what is kindly referred to as "deceptive advertising." There is a very simple reason for its success: People who have been frantically, though unsuccessfully, searching for something important to them will eventually reach the point where their thinking becomes muddled, and they, in their desperation, become highly suggestible. For example, if you allow a group of people to crawl around long enough in a desert without giving them water, their desperate, dehydrated minds will create an oasis, or at the very least, a drinking fountain.

The legendary King Midas's desire for gold was so great that one night, fatigued from counting and recounting his money, he asked the gods to grant that everything he touched might be turned to gold. His quest had so distorted his moneygrubbing little mind that he could no longer think rationally. "Yo! King, dude! Ya want a side of fries with that Mcgilded burger?"

It is at this level of nonrationality that I believe you'll find the majority of us hard-core power dieters. We'll not only buy, but believe (albeit temporarily) anything with the promise of a tiny tomorrow.

They know all about us rotundos, with our weaknesses and desperations. They also know the key words and how to manipulate them to our cumulative detriment. And it is this knowledge, in the wrong hands, my fleshy friends, that has become our nemesis! They barrage us with such obscure words as ***normal, average, beautiful, attractive, sexy, enticing, desirable,*** and myriad other equally nebulous adjectives that describe what we supposedly should be, but somehow haven't yet become. The words taunt us and prey on our human need to be accepted, until eventually, that need becomes a neurosis, and we'll try just about anything to (pardon the pun) fit in. At this point, as the saying goes, they got us where they want us.

Weekly we're confronted with a half a dozen or so different (not to mention contradictory) diets or weight-loss gimmicks that would appear, judging by the catchwords, to be identical. They're all *new, amazing, incredible, breakthrough* discoveries, with promises of *effortless, automatic weight loss, visible results in just two days,* and *fantastic results guaranteed, or your money back!*

I have a silly question. If they tell us right up front that these schemes are incredible, why do we insist on believing them? The only truly amazing thing about them is that we continue to be taken in! Visible results in just two days. Oh, come now! If (which, with gordos is most likely the case) you have been eating voraciously for the week prior to beginning this new, incredible weight-loss discovery, *any* limitation in that pattern will cause visible results. Try eating just two pizzas a night instead of your usual three, and I guarantee that within two days *your* bathroom scales will mysteriously reflect a reduction in weight too. Any professional dieter knows that the first few days of a diet are not the difficult ones. We always lose then, no matter what we try. It's the days that follow that try us! It will be my dying wish to see an ad say something like, "Visible results continued through the fifth and sixth days, followed by more visible results on the eleventh and twelfth days, and even more visible results on the ninety-ninth and one-hundredth days, and so on, *or your money back!*"

Or your money back, indeed! That's a safe offer if I've ever heard one! For those of us who have tried and failed so many diets already and find ourselves at the point of realizing that the automatic results are not forthcoming this time either, it would be sheer embarrassment to write requesting our money back. Why, that would be admitting to a company of complete strangers that we'd added yet another to our mounting list of failures—listen up now—*AND THEY KNOW THAT!*

Then there are those firsthand experience blurbs, attested to by twin sisters Ima and Ura Liar from Prevarication, Tennessee, complete with before and after pictures that by no stretch of the imagination could be the same people, because in the before shot they were obviously thirty or so years older than they were in the after shot! And, speaking of before and after pictures, let's get serious. Considering all the diets you've embarked upon over the years, exactly how many times did you have the forethought or, more to the point, the *guts* to have a before picture taken? And if you did, and you didn't cheat and make notes on the backs of the pictures, could you honestly tell the "befores" from the "afters?"

How about those old girdle ads that promised to take away inches instantly? Did you ever ask yourself where the inches went? There has to be a law of displaced matter that states that lard, when squeezed from its normal habitat, continues to shift until it reaches a place where it is no longer given resistance. In other words, out the top and the bottom of the girdle! It has to go somewhere. That fact always prevented me from buying one of those encase-the-entire-body girdles. I had horrible visions of adipose tissue seeping out like happens in a Stephen King story, in throbbing, grotesque blobs beneath my ankles and under my chin.

In my opinion, television is equally to blame. One morning I counted forty-four commercials between 10:00 and 12:00. Twenty-three of those were advertising either a food or a beverage of some sort. Of the remaining "nonfood" twenty-one, eight still showed people either preparing or eating food. This is all beginning to reek of mind control.

Remember that commercial where this hefty fella ate one tiny bowl of chili and said, "I can't believe I ate the whole thing!"? I always wondered why the heck not? One bowl? Come on, get serious. I know skinny people who can do that without even blinking an eye!

I've never hit myself on the forehead and exclaimed, "Wow! I could have had a V-8!" I'd simply add it (or anything else I might want) to my snack.

I see a well made-up anorexic on the tube wearing a bikini while lustily drinking a soda pop of the nondiet persuasion and am momentarily deluded into thinking that if I drink that same kind of pop, then of course, I too could be thin. But, as I come out of the fog, I remember I *do* and I'm *not!* I wonder what would happen to the sales of that particular beverage if the advertisers showed it like it really is: for example, *me* in a bikini drinking their product. Would that my weight could drop as fast as those soda pop sales would!

A recent TV jingle reveals to us that "There's a smile in every Hershey Bar." What they neglect to say is that there's also 200 calories and 10 grams of fat in that same little

Hershey Bar. All of a sudden there's not quite so much to smile about.

I think my favorite commercial was the old one that repeatedly flashed pictures of luscious, gooey, fattening things interspersed every so often with a picture of a diet pop, while in the background, someone sang, "NO, NO, NO, NO, NO! YES-YES, YES-YES!" to the tune of the "Blue Danube Waltz." By the time that damn thing was over, I'd forget what it was I was supposed to say "no" to, and what it was I was supposed to say "yes" to. I only knew for certain that I wanted something, *anything,* to eat.

We diet dabblers must never forget that masters of deception have a way with words. They don't necessarily tell lies. They can't—that would be false advertising, which we all know is illegal. But, they can and do choose words that are very ambiguous. For example, consider the following:

You too ...

Can Eat a Boston Cream Pie in a Closet, in Less than Five Minutes, Without Dirtying Utensils or Leaving any Telltale Signs and **Not Gain a Single Ounce!**

1. First, you must supply the chosen closet with a pan of hot, sudsy water, several towels, and a change of clothing—one size too large. Take with you also a plastic shower cap; the color is unimportant. Enter closet, slip all of your hair under the shower cap, check your watch, and begin.

2. Hold pie in your right hand (left, if you are so inclined), open your mouth as wide as you can—come on, you're alone, we know you can open it wider than that! That's better, now *shove* that pie into your mouth until you gag and all you can do is swallow. Of course you can't taste the pie, but that is not our purpose here; it never really is to closet eaters. What we want to do is eat voraciously while making everyone else believe we never eat a thing.

3. Now that you are finished with the pie, you will note that you have an uncomfortable cramped feeling in your stomach. Not to worry; that's normal. It will pass. All you need to do is burp, and that will happen shortly, possibly before you finish wiping that mess off of your face with the warm, sudsy water. Scrub-a-dub-dub; belch; dry. Now, slip quickly out of your protective plastic shower cap, and voilà! Check your watch, and it should be just ticking off the last seconds of your five minutes. Don't worry if you went over a bit, a little more practice and you'll be competing with the pros.

4. Now is the time to slip out of your by-now-too-tight garments and into the oversized ones you put in the closet before beginning this little experiment. You will notice that this new garment feels oh so much more comfortable than those silly little next-size-smaller numbers you had been wearing.

5. Now, for the best part: The weigh-in.
   (Of course this will have very little significance unless you had the forethought to weigh yourself before embarking on this ridiculous fiasco.)
   Step softly onto the scale, hanging on to something for support. Come on, no fair leaning! Now, glance down at the numbers, and, what to your curious eyes should appear? As promised, you did not, I repeat, *did not* gain *a single ounce.* You gained *sixteen* of the little lovelies.

Technically, honesty in advertising simply means coming through with what you promise. Be careful!

*****

5

Environmental Pollution in the Land of Milk and Honey

Resolutions: (1) Lose 100 pounds by

***January 1, 1970**—New Year's*
Resolutions: (1) Lose 100 pounds by
June, (2) Quit smoking,
(3) Let hair grow, (4) Write.

Ever since I studied psychology in college, I have been plagued with an uncontrollable habit of word association. The discouraging part is my associations almost invariably have their connections with food. For example, every time I see George Washington's face staring up at me from the front of a one dollar bill, my mouth waters for a bowl full of cherries. I hear Della Reese is starring in *Touched by an Angel,* and I immediately crave a peanut butter cup. Someone tells me they're a Quaker, and I long for an oatmeal cookie. I'm beginning to feel like one of Ivan Pavlov's dogs. The only difference between those Russian bowsers and me is that whereas they were conditioned to salivate at the sound of a bell, I have been trained to work up a little spit at the sound of just about anything.

If, for example, I were given a word-association test using the various holidays as cue words, some of my responses would look like this:

Easter .... egg
Thanksgiving .... turkey
Christmas .... goose

Or perhaps using states or cities as the cues:

Georgia .... peach
Maine .... lobster
London .... broil

This malady might be semi-understandable when you take environmental factors into consideration. What I like to call *foodspeak*[†] literally abounds in today's world.

Many people name their children after a loved one or for some historically famous person. They might scan books of given names to aid them in their selection. But there are those, who, I'm sure, must have discovered their children's names while scrutinizing a cookbook. These people, with reckless abandon and without the least bit of consideration for the possible subliminal repercussions to fat people, actually have the audacity to give their children edible handles like Candy, Stew, and Olive.

It is absolutely impossible for me to use the telephone directory and not get hungry. Gerkin, Rice, and Wiener are only three of the succulent surnames I found just skimming through the local phone book. If it were possible to film the stream of goodies my mind conjures up while I'm trying to find a phone number, it could be shown during intermission at a drive-in theater.

If you were to visit New York City, which, interestingly enough is known as "The Big Apple," you would no doubt run across people from countries called Turkey, Greece, Hungary, and Chile.

---

† For a comprehensive listing of "foodspeak" terms, refer to Appendix 1

A single glance at a city map assures me that I am far from the only food-oriented person around. In Denver, the city planners prepared a veritable gourmet's delight. People can choose to reside on such taste tantalizers as Elderberry Road, Filbert Court, and Peach Way, to name just a few. The city map reads like the menu at a buffet dinner!

We even categorize people with food labels. A person can be saucy or sweet, or have a sour disposition. Just imagine, I can eat a hunk of cheese while chatting intelligently with a hunk of a man!

If we carry this lunacy a bit further, we even find people falling into our basic food groups. Under meats, fish, and fowl, we might find a ham, a crab, or a turkey. Vegetables might consist of string beans, cool cucumbers, or couch potatoes. Dairy selections might include a good egg or a big cheese. We have a great variety of nuts and fruits to choose from, for example, a hayseed, a hard nut to crack, or a bad apple. To round out the diet, we have a varied list of carbohydrates, such as a sugar daddy, a little tart, and a fruitcake. And after breakfast, we must never forget to supplement our diets with a real pill.

One would think that associating people with food is deranged enough, but I turn the tables and also personify my grocery list. To illustrate, I will reveal a recurring fantasy of mine. I dream that I have a potluck dinner at my place, and my guest list includes some longtime friends: Colonel Sanders, Captain Krunch, Ronald McDonald, Dolly Madison, Lorna Doone, Chiquita Banana, Chef Boy-Ar-Dee, Aunt Jemima, Mama Celeste, Antipasto, Wendy, and the Hills Brothers. Even in the fantasy, I don't suffer heartbreak upon their departure, but heartburn.

Food indicators appear just about every place we look. Take music for example. The Beatles cut some of their albums under the Apple Records label. If we tune into an oldies station, we can hear selections by performers that called themselves things like Bread, Tuna, and Meatloaf. Our call-in requests might include "I Like Peanut Butter," "Blueberry Hill," or "Mean Mr. Mustard."

Perhaps you'd prefer to cut a rug, or shake a leg, in which case you might choose to perform the big apple, the cake walk, or the mashed potato.

Today's performers treat us food fetishists no better, what with their Cake, Brandy, and Red Hot Chili Peppers, but at least they do seem to have a narrower, perhaps healthier focus, leaning toward naming themselves after fruits and condiments. Witness Blind Melon, Fiona Apple, and Salt 'n Peppa.

But the music/food association doesn't stop there. Not by a long shot. Country & Western and Bluegrass musicians occasionally play an instrument known as the Jew's harp (too often carelessly pronounced "juice harp"), or they might perform the rhythmical hand accompaniment referred to as "ham bone." You can eat a drumstick or be a rhythm section with two of them. You can either play a flute or drink champagne from one. A bass is either a deep singing voice, or a pan-fried freshwater delicacy. You can weigh out your allowed minuscule portions of food on a scale, or you can read music from one. You have your salad fork, you have your tuning fork. People get drunk and play the spoons. And finally, when musicians get together informally to play music, guess what they call what they're doing? A *jam* session!

Football is one area that might appear at first glance to be free from food contaminations. However, if we take a closer look, we find this just isn't the case. The ultimate goal of some collegiate football teams, depending of course on their particular conference, is to be good enough to make it to either the Sugar Bowl or the Orange Bowl. Football injuries often involve a jammed finger or a pulled tendon in the back of the knee known as the hamstring. If a player or a coach makes an egregious error on the playing field, he earns a foul, which rhymes with fowl, which, when plucked and prepared properly turns into a picnic.

A famous exlinebacker for the Buffalo Bills, now even more famous because of a certain well-publicized double murder case, was nicknamed "The Juice." The Chicago Bears used to have a little fella on their team who went by the name of William "The Refrigerator" Perry. And on those occasions when they are performing well, the Denver Broncos have been affectionately called the "Orange Crush."

Then there's the movies and the television and the radio, which are apparently also out to sabotage the efforts of those of us who are trying desperately to avoid all thoughts of things that go gulp in the night (or morning, or afternoon). Consider if you will that at midday where I live, *National Public Radio* offers a classical segment entitled *Bachs Lunch.* Our children are bombarded on a daily basis with television episodes of *Lamb Chop, Beetlejuice,* and other children's fare having titles peppered with the names of food.

And speaking of food, a person could learn to cook, in the privacy of her own kitchen, just about anything her mouth happened to be watering for, thanks to the multitude of self-proclaimed cooking gurus like The Frugal Gourmet, Julia Child, Emeril Lagasse, Two Fat Ladies, and someone named Yan, who says he too can cook.

Those of us who are moviegoers have no reason to feel left out by any means. While we sit in the dark and stuff ourselves with our popcorn, Milk Duds, Jujubes, and a diet soda, we can enjoy all-time favorites, such as *Meatballs, Eating Raoul, The Three Musketeers,* and a seemingly endless list of Spaghetti Westerns starring an aging, but still very sexy Clint Eastwood.

And speaking of celebrities, I'm sure that if you keep your eyes open (you won't even have to look very hard), sometime or other you'll find yourself watching movies starring such famous names as Kevin Bacon, John Candy, or Joseph Bologna.

If you're the type who would rather just stay home and read, perhaps you could sink your teeth into *The Milagro Beanfield Wars, Fried Green Tomatoes, The Beans of Egypt Maine, The Grapes of Wrath,* or *The Brownie Handbook.* You could run to your local library and seek out books by famous authors such as Anne Rice, Joyce Carol Oates, or Salman Rushdie.

Everyday conversation, harmless as it may sometimes seem, is overflowing with trite expressions that refer to food and/or eating. For example look at the expressions "man does not live by bread alone" or "this job is a piece of cake," among many, many others. Lord help us, but even something as basic as money is variously referred to as sugar, berries, chips, lettuce, dough, cabbage, and bread!

Perhaps the possibility of seeking asylum from the assault in an untamed mountain forest has entered your mind. Don't waste your time. First of all, there probably isn't such a place anymore, and second, and more importantly, if there is, even in nature there is no refuge. Hidden within the birds, bugs, and beasts category, you can find honey bears, honey bees, peacocks, magpies, silver fish, fruit flies, butterflies, potato bugs, and tomato worms. Flora offers us sweet peas, honeysuckle, buttercups, asparagus grass, crab grass, and milkweed. Billowy clouds are often described as "cotton candy." Staring back at you from a clear night sky is the Milky Way, containing both a big and a little dipper and a moon that is purported to be made of green cheese.

Lest you were beginning to think (or hope) that this exposé on our mania for food-oriented labels must surely be coming to a close, I have one thing to say. *Au contraire!* Which, loosely interpreted, is French for fat chance! Wordsmiths that we are, we humans shamelessly even include animal waste products in our categorization. When no one's looking, you stick your finger in your nose, and if you're lucky, you pull out a big "goober," which Uncle Remus melodiously reminds us is another name for peanut. You sweat profusely then stand in a draft, and your skin becomes clammy. That gooey white substance that collects between your toes on a hot summer day has been cleverly dubbed toe jam. You throw up and some will say you have "tossed your cookies," "tossed your lunch," "fed the fish," or simply "blown grits."

Have you ever taken the time (then again, why would you?) to think about the various appellations created for feces? I have heard human solid waste called dingleberries and diarrhea referred to as "the green apple quick step."

Manure from a cow is called a cow pie. From a buffalo, we get buffalo chips. And a horse indiscriminately drops "prairie muffins" in the road, or, if you'd rather, "road apples" in the prairie.

If, after a late-night party, you're unfortunate enough (or low-down enough) to pass gas (a.k.a., let a popcorn or a beer fart) in a crowded elevator, someone is bound to squinch up their face in disgust and whine, "Hey, man, who cut the cheese?"

When their bladders are full, most normal people go into a bathroom and relieve themselves into a toilet "bowl." Lately I've begun to fear for my sanity, because even the word *commode* is starting to sound as though it could be a dessert . . . anyone for pie a-commode?

With all this in mind, I thought it might be interesting to recreate a typical day in the life of a fat girl who has once again bolstered the strength to embark upon yet another diet. Special attention should be paid to the numerous environmental food cues that continuously bombard her. I call this little commentary "The Insidious Disorientation of Candy Kane." (Don't reject the name as contrived so quickly—I once worked with a girl whose parents actually stuck her with that unfortunate moniker.)

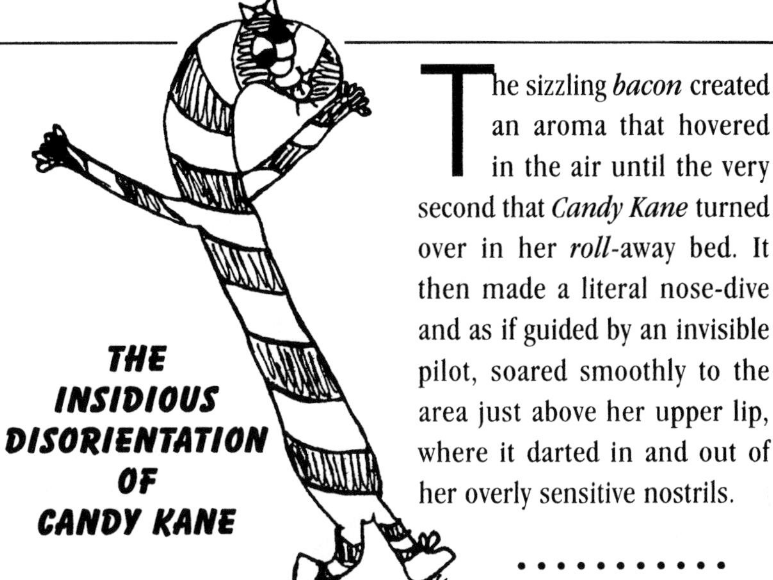

THE INSIDIOUS DISORIENTATION OF CANDY KANE

The sizzling *bacon* created an aroma that hovered in the air until the very second that *Candy Kane* turned over in her *roll*-away bed. It then made a literal nose-dive and as if guided by an invisible pilot, soared smoothly to the area just above her upper lip, where it darted in and out of her overly sensitive nostrils.

• • • • • • • • • • •

Candy opened her *almond*-shaped eyes. She swallowed hard as the tantalizing smell caused her mouth to begin to fill with saliva. Her stomach rumbled, demanding that she ***break*** the *fast. Candy,* still semiconscious with sleep, bolted up in bed, ready to comply with the silent orders she had just received. She winced as the sudden movement caused her too-tight *burgundy* nightgown to rub against her sunburned back. The pain jarred her into consciousness. Now fully awake, she remembered that today she was to begin yet another new diet. Panic gripped her as reason grappled with her insistent taste buds and grumbling stomach. Reason, outnumbered, was about to give way, when a ripple of determination forced its meager way to the surface. *"Coffee.* Just *coffee,"* she admonished herself.

Candy, apprehensive of the upcoming *food* battle, threw back the *cranberry*-colored bedspread, got out of bed, and stretched. She slipped her feet into her new, mail-order, *plum*-hued bedroom slippers, which sat on the *nutty* brown carpet next to her solid *walnut* dresser. She bent to pick up a couple of stray Styrofoam *peanuts* that must have fallen from the shipping box. *Candy*'s stomach growled.

She wandered sleepily into the kitchen, where *Ginger,* her *bean*pole of a roommate, was just sitting down to her breakfast of *eggs* scrambled with *mushrooms, bacon, oatmeal, toast* with *strawberry jam,* and *apricot nectar.* Looking very like the cat that just *swallowed* the canary, *Ginger* mumbled "Good morning" around a mouthful of *food.*

Candy stood helpless as her eyes zeroed in on the *feast* displayed before her on the *cherry* wood table. "Morning. *Coffee.* Just *coffee,*" she said.

"Say what?"

"I need some *coffee,*" explained *Candy.*

Ginger nodded toward the *chocolate* brown stove. "It just now finished percolating."

Candy opened the door of the *black walnut* cupboard and automatically reached for two *pumpkin*-colored *coffee* mugs. "Want some?"

"Mm hmm."

Candy filled the mugs with *coffee,* set the one without a *chip* down in front of *Ginger,* and took a seat in the *cream*-colored *bean*bag in the corner. She looked at *Ginger* for the first time that morning. "Holy *mackerel!* You're red as a *beet!*"

Ginger nodded. "I think we got too much sun yesterday. Your normally *olive* complexion looks like a *lobster* this morning."

"We probably shouldn't have used the *cocoa butter,"* said *Candy.*

"Or the *coconut* oil," offered *Ginger.*

Candy finished her *coffee* and went into the bathroom. She scrutinized her face in the mirror, discovering several new unsightly blackheads and realized if she wasn't careful, someone would start calling her *pizza* face. She wondered with envy why she hadn't been lucky enough to look more like *Ginger. Ginger* had *carrot* red hair and *avocado* green eyes. As if that weren't unfair enough, she had a *peaches* and *cream* complexion, due undoubtedly to her faithful use of *oatmeal* masque, followed by *honey lemon* face *cream.*

Candy brushed her teeth with *peppermint* toothpaste, *chip*ped away at her *tartar* buildup with *spearmint*-flavored floss, and rinsed her mouth, using a mouthwash containing essence of *cinnamon.* She washed her face with *avocado* cleansing *cream,* then looked at her *honey*-blonde hair in the mirror and decided it definitely needed a re*frosting,* which, for now, she'd have to put on the *back burner.* Just now she only had time for a shampoo. She scanned her cosmetic shelf and pondered a few minutes, trying to decide whether she should use the *apricot*-scented shampoo, the *apple,* or the *strawberry-kiwi.* Instead, she decided to use the one claimed to be made with *milk* and a mixture of various other *foodstuffs.* After she washed her hair, she applied a *honey-wheat germ* conditioner to ensure that her hair would be tangle free and as shiny as an *apple* from a teacher's pet.

While in the shower, *Candy* shaved her legs using *mint*-scented shaving *cream* and scrubbed herself all over with a *lime*-based deodorant soap. She jumped out of the shower, dusted herself with a *corn*starch-based powder, and splashed herself lightly with *honey*suckle perfume.

Once more at the mirror, she carefully put on makeup. She used *melon*-green eyeshadow, *orange* blusher to thin out her *meaty* cheeks, and *cola*-flavored lipstick.

Just then, *Ginger* knocked on the bathroom door. "You just about done?"

"Come on in. I'm almost famished—I mean, finished," answered *Candy.*

Ginger opened the bathroom door and steam gushed past her into the hallway. "God, it's just *roast*ing in here!"

"Not to me," said *Candy.* "In fact, I think it's downright *chilly.*" Then glancing quickly at *Ginger* in the mirror, she said, "this is totally off the subject, but what'd you think of that *turkey* who introduced himself to us on the beach yesterday?"

"Turkey?" argued *Ginger.* "Why, I was just pleased as *punch* with him. In fact, I thought that big *beefcake* was just as *sweet* as *pie!"*

"How could you think that?" *Candy* asked incredulously. "He was a real *Ding Dong.* All he did was talk about himself. I've never really liked anyone who felt *pressed* to *beef* up their life just to impress the next guy."

"I suppose that's *food* for thought," *Ginger* laughed, "but, come on, *Candy,* this sounds a little like *sour grapes* to me. He just wanted to *chew* the *fat* with us a little. But, then again, here's something for you to *chew* on. He did seem to pay more attention to me than he did to you."

"Get off of it! That *apple* polisher really must have pulled the wool over your eyes. Why, that *seedy* son-of-a-gun tried to *sandwich* himself between the two of us the entire day. I'll give it one week and I'll bet you'll find out what a *meatball* he really is. My advice is, just don't put all your *eggs* into one basket."

"Look, *Candy,* this really isn't worth your getting worked up into a *stew* over. If nothing comes of it, well, I guess that's just the way the *cookie* crumbles. Now, I have to get cleaned up, or I'll be late for work."

Candy grabbed her comb from the shelf under the mirror and returned to the kitchen. "God, I'm so hungry I could *eat* a house," she thought. Then aloud, "*coffee,* just *coffee.*" She poured herself another cup and carried it with her into the bedroom to get dressed. She looked into the closet at her new *lemon chiffon, spaghetti*-strapped dress. Today, she had an appointment to get her graduation picture taken, so she wanted to look really *peachy.* She looked at the floor of her closet and tried to decide whether she should wear her *bone* wedgies, the shoes made out of *marshmallow* leather, or maybe those that promised a *mushroom* walk. She wasn't really sure what that meant, but she guessed the shoes were supposed to be comfortable. She hoped so, in any case, because the photographer's studio was a mile's walk away down *Wheatberry* Street to *Strawberry* Drive. Anyway, they looked smart with the dress, so, if they turned out to be *weenies* in the comfort department, well, as the saying goes, you just can't have your *cake* and *eat* it too.

Once dressed, she stood in front of the mirror and attempted to twist her hair into a fashionable *bun.* When that didn't work, she began again and this time, carefully styled it into bouncing *banana* curls. Her creation complete, she stepped back to get a better view and smiled into the mirror. "Not too bad, if I squint," she said. "Marilyn Monroe, *eat* your heart out!"

Candy walked into the living room just as *Ginger* emerged from the bathroom wearing her red and white *candy*-striper uniform. Once again, *Candy*'s stomach gurgled.

Well, gotta *shake* the lead out," said *Ginger.* "I'll meet you back here after work and we'll do *dinner."*

"Wait, I'll walk with you to the *fork* in the road. I need to be at the photographer's by 9:00." *Candy* grabbed her copy of "The *Grapes* of Wrath" so she would have something to read in case she had to wait at the studio.

They had only gotten a couple of blocks away from home when *Candy* remembered, "Oh, *crackers!* I forgot to soak the dishes in *lemon* fresh Joy."

Ginger shrugged her shoulders. "Too late now. Anyway, as my *sweet* mama used to say, no use crying over spilled *milk."*

Candy felt hungry.

The waiting room at the studio was as crowded as *sardines* in a can when *Candy* arrived. Thinking that the room was just a little too *toasty* for her *taste,* she stood impatiently and waited for a place to sit down. She watched as a scantily clothed woman with *nutty*-brown skin, *strawberry*-blonde hair, and *raisin*-colored eyes stood up and sashayed through the back door to have her picture taken. "No doubt one of your basic *cheesecake* shots," *Candy* thought smugly to herself as she took the vacant chair. She started to open her novel when her eyes caught a glimpse of a magazine advertising an article on *Babe Ruth.* "Boy, that sounds good," she thought. Her stomach growled. "Maybe this article will explain why they named a baseball player after a famous *candy bar,"* she thought as she reached for the magazine. She really tried to read the article, but got only as far as the sportsman's name, when her mind created the vivid image of a *chocolate-coated nut roll . . .*

"Miss *Kane.* Miss *Kane!"* The voice was insistent. *Candy* blinked and shook her head, trying to dislodge the *sweet* thought that had kept her mesmerized. She looked at the clock. 10:45! How long had she been in that daze, anyway? Feeling as though she'd been caught with her hand in the *cookie* jar, *Candy* looked into the *milk*y eyes and *prune* face of the *salt*-and-*pepp*er haired receptionist, and her mouth watered.

"Miss *Kane,* Mr. *Burger,* the photographer, is waiting. If you don't hurry, I'm afraid we'll just have to go on to the next person. He is a busy man, you know."

Unable to take her eyes from the old woman's *liver* lips, and not wishing to upset the *apple* cart, *Candy* blurted, "Oh, no, please. I'm ready."

The old *crab* led *Candy* into a small, rather unexciting room containing a camera, several spotlights, and a cheap backdrop, in front of which she was asked to stand. A muffled voice came from under the black *cheese*cloth that was draped from the back of the camera. "Ready, Miss *Kane?* Now, say *cheese."*

Candy thought she heard what sounded like a small thread snap inside her *noodle*. A tic appeared suddenly in her *meaty, wine*-red, left cheek, just below her *glazed, toast*-brown, *almond*-shaped, eye. Then, as if from a great distance, she heard her own voice shrieking at the hidden photographer. "Why *cheese,* you *bean*-brain? Why not please, or trees? Why does it specifically have to be *cheese?* You know, you're really lucky I don't come over there and *punch* you in the *chops!* Or *jam* my fist into that *beer* belly of yours!"

With that, she ran wide-eyed and drooling from the photography studio, crossed the street without looking, almost causing a collision between an *orange* VW *rabbit,* an *ice cream* truck, and a police cruiser with a *cherry* on top, and *duck*ed into the five and dime, where without deliberation, she purchased a pound and a half of *chocolate bridge mix.* This, she *devoured* in a matter of *seconds,* and with the final *taste*less swallow, came an all-too-familiar overwhelming depression. Another failure! She trudged home, head hung low like a puppy that has just been severely reprimanded.

Once home, *Candy* felt comforted by the familiar surroundings. "Get ahold of yourself, girl," she lectured. "So you broke down. Go on from here. Just don't let yourself think about *food* and everything will be okay." Hopeful that music might calm her nerves, she turned on the radio, sat back, and closed her eyes to listen. The first sound she heard was the smooth voice of Nat King Cole singing, "Bring back those lazy, hazy, crazy days of summer. Those days of *soda,* and *pretzels,* and *beer . . ." Candy* felt her *clam*my hands clenching into fists. She sat up angrily and tuned in another station. When she found a soft instrumental, she felt herself relax a little, and once again she leaned back to enjoy the music. She just barely heard the quiet knock at her door. Resentfully, she pushed herself up, went to the door, and opened it.

Two little girls *dressed* in *Brownie* uniforms stood there waving a selection of *cookies* in her face. Without thinking, *Candy* started to reach for her purse, then suddenly, she *waffle*d. "Go peddle your poison somewhere else, you rotten little *shrimps!"* she shouted, abruptly slamming the door in the two horrified little faces.

Candy's knees suddenly felt like *jelly,* and she collapsed weakly against the door. "Poor little *dumplin's,"* she thought. "I just have to pull myself together." Wearily, she sat back down in her chair, waiting for some soothing music, but instead a commercial for a *fast food* restaurant reminded her that she in fact "deserved a break today." In order to drown out the temptation of the words, *Candy* hummed a single note as long and as loud as she possibly could.

She looked out the window. The sun had already set. The peaceful darkness beckoned her to the porch to indulge in the breeze and night sounds. She *drank* in an enormous breath of the cool, crisp air and looked up at the sky. As she did, she heard a flight-for-life *eggbeater* overhead and a guitar plucking the *"Orange* Blossom Special" on the radio inside. Just then a *honey*bee buzzed past her face in the darkness. She felt another snap as the big *dipper* drizzled *chocolate* over the *Milky Way,* and the man in the *green cheese* moon laughed down at her, mocking. *Candy* shuddered, shrugging her *beefy* shoulders in final defeat.

When *Ginger* arrived home later that night, she found *Candy* sitting cross-legged in a corner quietly eating her *spaghetti*-strap dress. When she was interviewed afterward at the hospital about the possible cause of *Candy*'s collapse, *Ginger* took a swig from her can of *soda pop* and said, "I really don't know what happened to the *sweet* little *fruitcake.* I guess she just finally went *bananas!*"

*****

6

Sex and the Pringle Girl

(or Just Where Does a Fat Person Get Her Jollies?)

April 1, 1973—Today I'm finally thin! 130 pounds, sexy, and beautiful. Four guys called me for a date. My life is changing before my very eyes! April fools, fool! Nine weeks till summer ... Get on the stick, fatso!

I once heard someone on television make the following declaration: "I've got a great new diet! You can eat whatever you want, but you must eat every meal with naked fat people!" That might just work, not only for obvious reasons, but because you'd no doubt burn a good number of calories trying to find a fat person willing to sit calmly with you and eat *anything,* let alone several courses in the buff.

Although I understand there is an obscure faction out there that purportedly prefers to play around with portly people, I can't help but hold them suspect. They're probably just morbidly curious skinny folks who wonder not only what it would be like to be *with* a fat person but what it would be like to *be* a fat person. Or maybe they're just sexually deprived, ergo, horny, fat people who are so self-conscious they couldn't bear to be with anyone who wasn't equally orgasmically challenged. These people go around making unsubstantiated claims that because a person is king-sized, it follows that they have more to be sensuous with, and that under all these folds and flaps can still be found frustrated, but fully-functioning equipment. Or it might be they're just normal folks who truly do believe that fat is beautiful. I, however, do not fall within the category of people who feel that way.

For me, naked and fat is a mortifying combination of circumstances. Whenever it happens to me, one phrase keeps flashing through my mind: "My kingdom for an overblouse!" In this situation, lights are your enemies, reflections your foes. Thomas Edison suddenly becomes the Marquis de Sade. You feel that if you (or anyone) just never had to see your fat again, everything would be all right. That is, if you could ignore the myriad other reminders that continually harass you.

For example, feeling the uppermost part of your thighs (often insensitively referred to as saddlebags) hanging over either edge of a normal-sized straight-back chair, or realizing that not one, but a *pair* of tires has stealthily oozed over the top of the waistband of your plus size designer jeans. Or maybe you feel an untimely burst of fresh air as the armpit of your blouse rips, or the nylon zipper of your pants begins to open from the middle. Perhaps you feel your cheeks flush as someone mistakes the sudden rip emanating from the crotch of your leggings for a clap of thunder.

Naked and fat creates the same frustrations as I can only guess that voluptuous and clothed would evoke. Just once, I'd like to give naked and voluptuous a try! Sometimes, when I'm besotted and every light in the world is off, I can pretend that I come close. But, light a single match, and instantly my fantasy dissolves. Some people have small shadows . . . mine looms huge and overbearing on the wall!

As a result of these drawbacks, you can imagine that pleasurable sex begins to resemble Shakespeare's sleep, in that it becomes "a consummation devoutly to be wished!" For the most part humiliated by the experience, I used to think I would become slave to whatever man happened to be present when everything went right. By "right," I meant, I would be at 149 pounds and still losing rather than at 200 pounds and gaining. It would be during a blackout in New York, we would be fresh out of matches, with only champagne to sustain us, and there would be a total eclipse of the sun the following morning, lasting at least long enough for me to escape, while I and the world were still clothed in darkness.

In lieu of the real thing, on occasion I tend to nurture a vivid and creative, perhaps a tad overactive, imagination. And, by the way, I'm convinced that those erotic scenes that my mind conjures up will never be available to me unless I somehow manage to get in with the thin crowd.

I would, however, like to take this time to dispel a nasty rumor. I've read entirely too often that food is a sex substitute for fat people. I might go so far as to admit that some of us might lean toward hedonism. After all, none of the five senses is forgotten in regards to pleasurability when it comes to food. Take, for example, a simple Italian dinner of a vegetable salad tossed with a creamy dressing, lasagna, garlic bread, and spumoni ice cream. Each of our senses are individually gratified by this meal. Take sight, to begin with. The meal is a veritable rainbow of colors. It also smells heavenly, as the tomato-oregano-basil-Parmesan-garlic-laden aroma wafts temptingly beneath our nostrils. It sounds mouthwatering as we chew the crisp vegetables, crunch on a crusty piece of garlic bread, smack our lips around yet another forkful of cheese-filled, gooey lasagna, and slurp spoonfuls of the slightly melted spumoni. We feel the various textures and temperatures tantalize out mouth: hard, soft, smooth, crisp, creamy, hot, warm, cold. Our taste buds want to squeal with delight at just the right combination of tart, bland, spicy, and sweet. There you have it. The five senses—sight, smell, sound, touch, and taste—with this meal, not one has been denied the pleasure of its own unique experience.

Yet, I must object when it comes to the ridiculous implication that the minds of fat people are so distorted that they stoop to using food as a sex substitute! (No, Mr. Mason, those cracker crumbs in my bed do *not* constitute proof, they are merely circumstantial evidence!) Rather, I submit that it is the culinary verbiage that has evolved over the years to describe sexuality that has a subliminal influence on our desire to eat!

Think back for a minute. What did you call male genitalia when you were little and afraid, not to mention embarrassed, to say the word *penis?* My friends and I called it a wiener. When I grew up a little, the thing's moniker graduated to salami. When we first realized there was a visible difference between boys and us, we little girls used to band together on a neighbor's porch and chant at the passing boys, "you've got the hot dogs, we've got the buns!" It would be many years before I learned about the Freudian symbolism of that little chant. Then, we were simply talking about the way things looked.

Even today, there is a slang term for female genitalia that is reminiscent of a chocolate dessert . . . *brownie*. Tell the truth now, what do you think of when you hear the word *nuts? Cream?* What does a virgin have that an ex-virgin does not? Why, a cherry, of course! All we need now is a couple scoops of ice cream, and we'd have the makings of a fabulous sundae. How 'bout it, getting a little hungry yet?

What about all those endearing terms we have for our loved ones? *Honey, sugar, sweety pie, dumplin', pumpkin.* To court someone is to spoon, for gosh sakes! Didn't they used to call women tomatoes? And men, pieces of meat? How about forbidden fruit? I have a good friend who refers to a sexually desirable woman as "tasty." A naked person is said to be "in the raw." We are each said to have a sexual appetite, of all things. Breasts of a small-chested woman are referred to by some as "fried eggs," and somewhat more ample breasts are often compared to melons.

You can peel a potato, and you can peel off your clothes. You can turn on your stove, or you can turn on your mate. You can eat out at a restaurant, or you can eat out at home. You've got your main course, you've got your intercourse. If a woman gets pregnant, some say she's been bred (sounds like?). How about the old roll in the hay that put the bun in the oven? A woman can get a yeast infection, or, if she's indiscriminate in choosing a sex partner, she could get crabs. Even the word *mastication* sounds suspiciously like *masturbation!* So, I ask you. Is there really any wonder that some of us get a little excited about food?

*****

7

Heavy Hands Are Not Overweight Migrant Workers

__August 23, 1977__—I'm twenty-eight today. Do I feel older? No. Different? No. I got an overblouse from Judy and a box of candy from the people at work. I wonder if they planned that? I put the blouse on and ate the entire box of candy. Monday I went to the doctor for a breast exam. Why in hell do they find it necessary to weigh you in for that? One hundred ninety-one pounds of ugly fat on the deadly accurate scale! If I allow three pounds a shoe, two pounds for the dress...

Thus far I have avoided the topic of exercise. I've also spent the better part of my life avoiding participation in anything that even resembled exercise. I've often found it to be just too damned embarrassing. Don't get me wrong, I could squat, I just couldn't thrust. I remember that during physical fitness testing in high school, we were required to do a timed arm hang. Once I broke the low record at Iowa City High School by collapsing breathlessly to the floor in exactly 1.2 seconds.

Before it was fashionable, one of my sisters and I made big plans to try jogging to get into shape. At that time, we lived in the country in Indiana, and the road we decided to jog on had virtually no traffic after 10:00 p.m. We decided to jog at that hour, the pitch darkness being the final determining factor. Wouldn't you know it, the very first night we went out, not one, but *six* cars drove down that "deserted" road, the occupants gaping at us as though they thought they might be witnessing criminals escaping from the scene of a crime. It was humiliating jiggle-jogging down the road like we were. I lowered my head, pulled up my gray sweat-suit hood, and headed back home. I couldn't get there fast enough.

For much of my life, the only exercise I got was writing and rewriting my exercise program. I know that doesn't sound like much, but I was one of those people who could get winded just changing the channel on my television set. In those days, of course there was no such thing as remote control. Nope, no conveniences for us. We actually had to stand up, walk all the way across a ten-by-ten room to the television set, and *twist a knob!* The same went for volume control. Yup, in the old days, we really had to work for our entertainment.

It's like I'm caught between that rock and that hard place you hear so much about. I hardly ever swim because I'm so fat, and I'm so fat because I hardly ever swim. Oh, I've tried it once or twice, and I even kind of like it, but as I said before, these things can be embarrassing. One time I displaced so much water when I dived into a municipal pool that an unsuspecting sunbather threatened to sue me for attempting to drown her.

Another time, I terrified a toddler by simply sliding down a swirly slide. He looked up to the top of the slide as I, in my *so-called* flaw-concealing, black, skirted bathing suit, was scootching toward the edge, and saw what to him must have looked a little like Free Willemina attempting her escape. His eyes bulged to the size of hubcaps, as he attempted a slow-motion dash through the water, trying to get as far away from the bottom of the slide as his scrawny little legs could take him. His horrified scream, "Look out!!!" echoed as only a child's scream can in an indoor recreation center swimming pool.

All eyes were on me as I plunged deeply into the water at the bottom of the slide, sorely regretting the fact that it wouldn't be long until I'd have no choice but to resurface.

*****

My husband and I spent close to a thousand dollars on one of those cross-country skiing machines. You know, the one where the television ad shows us willing-to-try-just-about-anything viewers an intimate close-up shot of this couch potato's belly hanging precariously over the waistband of his BVDs? As this brave person skis on the ski machine, that belly of his just disappears and turns into a veritable washboard before our very eyes!

Well, my kids are pretty normal. Like the rest of us, they tend to believe what they see with their very own eyes. So, the first day I climbed onto my ski machine and struggled to look the least bit coordinated, my youngest stood there staring at my belly, no doubt expecting to see it disappear as quickly as the famous TV tummy had. When it didn't, she gave me a worried look and said, "Mommy, you must be doing it wrong." Oh, out of the mouths of babes . . .

I have a friend who bought a treadmill, set it up in front of her television (as a ploy to guarantee she'd use it), and walked on it faithfully every day, until one morning the beam across the ceiling in the room below where she exercised fell rumbling to the floor, apparently shaken loose by the vibrations of her exercise. I'll tell you, *some* people will do just about anything to get out of exercise!

I've tried group aerobics classes, both high- and low-impact as well as the step-up programs. I love the music. But I hate the mirrors, I hate very obviously being the only person in the entire rec center who actually needs to be there, and I hate the fact that I sweat buckets while everyone else barely even develops a slight sheen. And this all happens while I'm still in the locker room attempting to squeeze into a plus-size sliver of spandex that downright refuses to expand any further.

Out in the exercise room, once again I love the music and once again hate the mirrors and I hate the fact that I'm the only one in class who begins gasping for breath like a beached large-mouthed bass. And *this* all transpires while we're still in the middle of the warm-up exercises.

Since group grunting didn't seem to be my cup of tea, I decided to try my hand at the various home versions. On any given day, beginning at 5:00 a.m. and running through 8:30 a.m., I can privately tune in to *Cory Everson's Gotta Sweat, Everyday Workout, Fitness Beach, Denise Austin's Daily Workout, Kiana's Flex Appeal, Homestretch, Bodyshaping, Crunch Fitness, Fit TV, Co-Ed Training, Sit and Be Fit* (my personal favorite), and *Perfect Parts.* Okay, so there's lots to choose from, but get real. Who in their right mind gets up at 4:30 in the morning to get ready to exercise? And if you try to, and you happen to have a dog or kids, you don't get to exercise anyway, because the dog or the kids will hear you the very second you get out of bed and will get up and want to be fed, dressed, read to, or let out to pee.

Okay, I found an excuse why before-dawn-television-torture wouldn't work for me, so I went out and bought a Richard Simmons video aerobics tape, a Susan Powter video exercise tape, and a Jane Fonda audio walkout tape. On the positive side, with these videos at least I don't feel like the only (Let's see, what is the politically correct term they're calling us these days? Oh yeah!) *ample* or *plus* size person in existence. But I gotta tell ya. I'm still a long way from being convinced that *this* big is really all *that* beautiful.

I do get out there and walk once in a while with my dog and Jane, but not often enough for me to have experienced anything resembling positive results. The sister I jogged with on that long ago memorable occasion has succeeded; she actually has achieved those seemingly illusive positive results. She sold her car, walks or rides her bike wherever she goes, and is jogging almost daily and eating nutritious food and enjoying it. She looks absolutely wonderful, and she's a real boon to my all-but-faded hopes of eventual success. Seeing her makes me at least want to keep trying. After all, I came from the same gene pool as she did, didn't I? So I figure, with persistence and a lot of luck, I might one day be one of those skinny people I have mentally shoved a thousand times down an elevator shaft.

*****

8

Cold Turkey

June 1, 1980*—Refer to entries of August 23, 1962; January 30, 1965; May 14, 1966; June 10, 1967; January 1,1970; April 1, 1973; and August 23, 1977.*

Over the years, I've tried egg diets, banana diets, tomato diets, grapefruit diets, rice diets, high protein, low protein, high carbohydrate, low carbohydrate, pills, counting fat and fiber grams, and counting calories. (I have a rather morbid fantasy regarding calorie counters. I envision this minuscule numbers man sitting atop my shoulder counting every calorie as I eat it. He succumbs to exhaustion midway through the first meal of his assignment.) I've tried weight-loss clinics and even born the humiliation of wearing a plastic pig on my lapel for the heinous crime of gaining a couple of pounds. I've tried fasting, liquid diets, and candy appetite suppressants with tea. I've even tried eating what I want, when I want. I could just never quite figure out how to know for sure when it was time to stop. Once I wanted to see how much I could lose in a day if I ate nothing at all. I gained three pounds. And why wouldn't I? Feeding off of my own body for a day surely provided my system with a diet far higher in fat content than I would ever have been able to achieve by mouth. I tried listening to subliminal tapes, but no matter how deep was the trancelike state I managed to achieve, I just couldn't help laughing when I heard the soft voice instructing me to repeat the mantra, "I–am–at–my–*per*fect–weight."

Once I actually considered getting my stomach stapled but chose against it when I realized how much adipose tissue the surgeon would have to slice through just to get the stapler to my stomach. I decided it would be better if I lost a little weight before having that particular surgery.

Several years ago, I had been trying to find a new and different diet, hoping for the one with magic. I thought I'd been hiding my lard pretty well, when, to my enormous humiliation, an extremely overweight friend mentioned that he'd noticed my blouse looked tighter on me than it had the last time he'd seen me wear it. Shamed by this encounter, I was determined to find that magic diet. Tomorrow.

I have a terrible knack for developing habits in just about everything I do. My I-have-to-go-on-a-diet habit is a very involved one that begins with the re-realization that I am fat. Next, I panic with *tomorrow* at hand and dash madly down the aisles of the nearest supermarket, following my nose to the junk food displays. I ignore all speed limits returning to my apartment and pant as I run up the stairs, praying no one sees me. I lock the door securely behind me, pull the drapes shut, and dive double-fisted into the bags of poison and eat it all, not even bothering to take the time to cook those things that are best, by most standards, at least warmed up a little. I believe the technical term for what I do is *binge*. I've never followed up with a forced purge, although afterward I certainly always *feel* like throwing up. After expending so much energy chewing, slurping, and gulping, I'm exhausted and all I want to do is sleep. But lying down, I find it difficult to drift off, because I get heartburn if I lay on my back, and it hurts too much to lay on my stomach. The next morning, I get up, take care of all biological needs, and before taking even the smallest sip of water, I step gingerly onto the scales. Weaving slowly from left to right, forward to back, I try futilely to make the number staring up at me get smaller.

After the binge that followed my fat friend's unsolicited comment, I began my routine as was customary. Aghast at the fact that I weighed more than I ever had, I scurried to my closet and pulled out my personal collection of all the diets that had ever put into print. I had purchased them all, tried them all, failed them all, yet here I was again, going back to them as if I thought this time they would make me thin. Balderdash! It wasn't those diets that had failed, it was me. Any one of them could work, if only I would. With this not so profound thought in mind, I decided to create my own diet . . . the one that would work for me. I would eat a paragraph from each of those diets while drinking a cup of hot coffee or tea twenty minutes before each meal. It just had to work. Who could be hungry after eating so much crow?

I had a good friend in college who would *remember* that she hadn't eaten anything for three days. She didn't feel hunger, and at the time, I envied her that capability. She was very thin, and at 5'8" and 78 pounds, she was only beginning to see that she was too thin. I remember joking with her that if we could only melt ourselves together and divide the result in half, then maybe we'd both be a little happier about our weight. It turns out my friend was anorexic and for the longest time believed she weighed too much. She would actually look in a mirror and, rather than see the skeleton that stood there, she saw a fat person staring back at her.

She came from a very competitive East Coast family, and her parents were extremely proud of her two older sisters, who were models. My friend was desperate to get some of that love. She almost starved herself to death before her family got her some help. When I saw her in the hospital, she looked like a skeleton with skin. And at twenty-one years old, she was not allowed to have matches or a fingernail file, because the doctors were afraid she'd hurt herself with them. It was then I stopped wishing I could be like her and feel no hunger. Although I realized that we both had eating disorders, I didn't understand hers. I didn't want to have hers. Suddenly, although I didn't really understand it either, at least I felt secure with my own eating disorder. I was familiar with it. It was a known quantity, a lifelong friend. But I took very little comfort in that fact.

I have a friend who had a roommate in college whom she always wanted to be like. The roommate was smart, and pretty, and funny, and my friend envied the fact that she could get by with just coffee for breakfast and steak for dinner two or three times a week. My friend has recently seen this ex-roommate and she is no longer pretty, or funny. Now she suffers from osteoporosis and looks like she's just come out of a concentration camp. My friend doesn't envy her any more.

I once worked with a woman who honestly looked like a Barbie Doll. She was tall, thin, had big blond hair and an itsy-bitsy waist. She even wore skintight pants and spiked high heels. For a while some of us were jealous of her ability to eat anything she wanted and still look like that. We later came to realize it was the fact that after stuffing everything else down her throat, she'd follow with her fist, and it was the purging that was keeping her thin.

In 1996, widely publicized horror stories of short-term memory loss and leaky bowel syndrome notwithstanding, I tried desperately to convince my doctor to write me a prescription for that new fen-phen drug "cocktail" (a combination of the drugs Pondimin [fenfluramine] and phentermine) that I had been hearing so many success stories about. He refused to do it, citing literature he'd read saying that the drugs could produce *minor* side effects, for example, the possibility of users contracting a fatal lung or heart disease. Needless to say, since I was desperate enough to ask him to write the prescription in the first place, I was miffed when he refused, and even considered going to another doctor who had prescribed the cocktail for a friend of mine.

I stopped being miffed in September 1997, when the FDA ordered two diet drugs, one of them Pondimin, off the shelves because it seemed that about *one-third* of the people who had used the drugs had developed damaged and bleeding heart valves. Whew! Thanks, Doctor Pinto! I probably owe you my life.

Although I have yet to enjoy long-term success with any of the plans I've attempted, I still prefer to look on the bright side. I haven't tried everything yet.

There's still acupuncture, wiring my jaws shut, and liposuction. We'll see. I guess I'm saving them for more desperate times.

Lack of long-term weight-loss success aside, I have to say that reading so much diet literature has broadened my knowledge immensely. Among other things[†] I've learned that

---

† For an extended list of things I've learned about myself, refer to Appendix 2

I either eat too much, or I don't eat enough; that I was either born with a fat gene, or I contracted the recently exposed fat virus; and that I either want people to like me for who I am inside, or I actually hate who I am inside.

In addition to the array of tidbits I've learned about myself, I've also accumulated a wealth of information about the world of weight loss.† Take for example the mutually exclusive (but possibly useful) facts that calories don't count, or they do; exercise either increases your appetite, or it takes away your desire to eat; and you should either weigh yourself once a week, or you should throw your bathroom scales away. With all this vital, straightforward information at our fingertips, it really is quite a mystery why any of us remain confused.

One of my sisters once suggested that I use all of the information I've accumulated to start what I could call the "Doublechin Diet of the Month Club." New members would get the first four diets free but have to agree to buy one diet a month for the rest of their lives. Sounds like it could be profitable, but, then I'd probably be tempted to join the club myself and end up depleting all my profits.

*****

† For an extended list of the world of weight loss, refer to Appendix 2

9

Face the Fat

February 8, 1989—*Today I gave birth to one of the two most beautiful little girls in the world. Her name is Traci. Two and a half years ago I gave birth to the other one. Her name is Tessa. I never lost the 30 pounds I gained when I was pregnant for Tessa, or, for that matter, the 20 I gained when I quit smoking when I was pregnant for her. So here I am, saddled (saddle-bagged?) with all those pounds plus the 20 I gained this time. But hey, just look at my beautiful daughters . . . ain't I the lucky one?*

My daughters don't like it when I say I hate the way I look or when I wonder aloud if the new Kohl's department store has a fat lady section. I think they're wise beyond their years though, because at times like those, they never fail to point out something positive: "Mommy, you just have big muscles," or "Mommy, you're really pretty," or "Mommy, at least you have really soft hair," or "Mommy, you should be happy you're not as big as some people I've seen," or "Mommy, you are really smart," or "It's okay, you're still the best mommy in the world." And although it makes my heart swell with love for them when they say those things, there's a big part of me that's saying, "Yeah, yeah, yeah. I may be all those things, but I'm *still* fat!"

But, since I don't want to sound like a total whiner here, I think it's important that I point out that although being fat isn't necessarily a bowl full of cherries, it isn't always all bad either. I've thought about this a lot and, after taking a long, hard look at the situation, I've discovered that there really are some positive aspects of living large. For example, if you're overweight, you probably start a diet once every couple of days, so, like me, you are probably aware that the current trend in diets is to stress low-calorie, low-fat meals. Now, if you think about it, there's a real advantage to being fat and on a diet, when you compare the time and energy you'll spend cooking a full-calorie, full-fat meal versus a low-calorie, low-fat meal. Take, for example, that lasagna we subjected all of our senses to on a previous adventure.

Your Basic Full-Fat, Full-Calorie Lasagna

Ingredients:

1 pound hamburger (approximately 50% lean)
1 small onion, chopped fine
1 glove garlic, minced
1 pound can Italian-style crushed tomatoes

1 8-ounce can tomato sauce
1 6-ounce can tomato paste
1 6-ounce can of water
2 tablespoons parsley flakes
2 tablespoons sugar
1 tablespoon basil leaves
1 tablespoon oregano leaves
1 teaspoon salt
1 pound creamed cottage cheese
1 egg
1 cup grated Parmesan cheese (divided)
¾ pound grated mozzarella cheese
8 ounces lasagna noodles, cooked and well drained.

Method:

Cook and stir hamburger, onion, and garlic in a large saucepan until meat is brown and vegetables are tender. Drain off excess fat. (Would that it were so easy!) Add Italian tomatoes, tomato sauce, tomato paste, water, parsley, sugar, basil, oregano, and salt. Heat to boiling, stirring occasionally. Reduce heat and simmer uncovered 1 hour until sauce thickens.

Heat oven to 350°.

Mix cottage cheese, egg, and ½ cup of Parmesan cheese together in a bowl.

Lightly oil a 13x9x2-inch baking pan. Spread a little meat sauce on the bottom of pan and reserve ½ cup for a thin top layer. Then layer lasagna noodles, remaining meat sauce, mozzarella cheese, and cottage cheese mixture; repeat three times. Spread reserved meat sauce over the top and sprinkle with the remaining ½ cup of Parmesan cheese. (Take a swig of your favorite liquid and wipe that sweat from your brow with a clean paper towel.)

Bake uncovered for 45 minutes. Let stand 15 minutes after removing from oven before cutting into squares. (If you're still awake, serve with buttered, toasted garlic bread.)

Now, if you modify this recipe to simply cut out the fat and most of the calories you have:

Your Basic Reduced-Fat, Reduced-Calorie Lasagna

Ingredients:

1 pound can Italian-style crushed tomatoes

1 dry bread crust

Method:

Open tomatoes and transfer to microwavable bowl. Heat on high for 45 seconds till warmed through. Take bowl and bread crust to table. Close your eyes and use a great deal of imagination.

Don't like to cook? That's okay. There are other positive things about carting around all this excess adipose tissue. For example, unlike all those Twiggy wannabes out there, *we* don't have to wonder what it's like to have cleavage, nor will we ever have to pay some overpriced plastic surgeon to provide us with some. Also, unlike the willowy ones, we don't have to worry about getting fat. We already are. And, face it, if there ever is a famine, we stand a better than average chance of coming out of it alive. And just what about those skinny minnies? Do you think *they* sleep easy at night knowing how slim (so to speak) their chances are?

Oh, all right, so in the United States, in this day and age there's not a whole lot of likelihood that there will be a famine any time soon. Maybe that wasn't the best example. So, what about when your kids start to grow up? If you're fat, it's less likely that they will be bugging you to borrow your clothes all the time. Unless of course your kids have picked up a few of your bad habits and they happen to be fat too. But look on the bright side, if that's the case, then they, like you, will have a built-in excuse for why people don't like them, don't invite them to parties, don't hire them, or if they do get hired, why they never get promoted—they're fat. Normal-sized people don't have this luxury. Instead they are forced to consider the very grim possibility that maybe they just aren't likeable or hireable or promotable.

So you don't go in for that "poor me" attitude anymore? Good for you! It is sort of a waste of time, isn't it? But I'm here to say there are *still* some positive aspects of being a heavyweight. For example, we don't have to concern ourselves with keeping up with the latest fashion trends ... after all, they don't even *make* them in our size. We can just stick with the "slenderizing" basic blacks we wore last year.

Fewer choices, fewer headaches, fewer expenditures. And while we're on the subject of spending money, we queen-sized ones will probably never spend exorbitant sums on depilatories and those painful waxes that are said to spruce up our "bikini areas" either.

Speaking of swimming, have you ever thought about the fact that you could never be arrested for skinny-dipping? And even if by some chance you were, it's highly unlikely that the charge would hold up in court, because even your basic ho-hum lawyer ought to be able to get you off on what would seem like a rather obvious technicality. ("Your Honor, I object on the grounds of reasonability. If you'll take just one look at my client, and not even a very close one at that, I'm sure you'll agree that it is technically, not to mention physically, impossible for her to have committed the crime of skinny-dipping. Fatty-dipping sans clothing, perhaps, but, with something less than all due respect, Your Honor, I remind you she has been charged with *skinny*-dipping. I see no logical choice here but to drop all charges against her.")

And here's something else I'll bet you never thought about. If you're overly ample, it's not very likely that you'll ever get a reputation for sleeping around. Even if someone were to start such a nasty rumor, just how many people do you think would believe it anyway? Would you? Would your significant other? And speaking of significant others, if you have one and you're fat, do you think he's ever going to humiliate you in public by calling you his "little woman?" Of course he won't! In fact, I think we should all just stop counting our calories and fat grams and start counting our blessings, because if we were thin there would probably be times when we would think we had to put up with that kind of sexist, derogatory treatment! Not so for us fatties!

As a result of (or in spite of) realizing that there might be a different way of looking at things and that living large doesn't have to be a bad thing, there is a growing faction out there who have decided to lighten up in another way. Call it adipose acceptance, people in support of cellulite, or whatever you like, these brave people have decided that Fatty, Fatty Two-by-Four *can* get through the kitchen door, even if it requires a little ingenuity, like slathering petroleum jelly on the doorjambs.

* * * * *

10

Survival of the Fattest

April 1, 1995*—I just read in the paper that now leading scientists believe that obesity is caused by genes. Is this another April fools joke? It certainly makes for a handy excuse, but I guess I'll choose to believe that, like most of the other stuff I've read, this isn't true either. If it were, I'd never even have a shot at being thin, now would I? I don't think I could face that—life without hope.*

June 25, 1996*—I begrudgingly went to the swimming pool at the rec center with the kids today. They begged me to go down the twirly slide. When I sat down at the top of the slide and started down, I caught the look of terror on the face of a little boy who was standing near the bottom of the slide. I felt as though I was moving in slow motion, as he gaped at me, and displaying unmitigated horror, he screamed, "LOOK OUT!!" You might say I made quite a splash. And for the umteenth time, I vowed never to wear a swimsuit again.*

***April 12, 1997**—I saw in the paper that a virus (specifically adenovirus 36 or Ad-36) known to cause obesity in animals has now been tied to weight problems in human beings, which some say raises the possibility that some people "catch" obesity and that it might actually be an infectious disease. Yeah, right! Fat chance! But, just on the off chance it's true, I might have to check into inoculations.*

It seems that no matter what I try and no matter how strong my convictions are at the outset of any dietary endeavor, my powers of rationalization come to the fore and invariably prove victorious. And in the end it seems the only thing thin about me is my patience.

I once tried pasting a picture of a grotesquely obese person on my refrigerator door. Theoretically, I should have taken one look at that picture and not wanted to eat anything. What happened is, I looked at the picture, said to myself, "Hell, I'm not *that* fat," opened the refrigerator, and proceeded to stuff myself until I *felt* that fat.

On the flip side, there is the little trick of taping a picture of a very shapely girl on your cupboard door. This is intended to shame you into not eating. I tried this, but rather than shame me, the picture depressed me, so in order to make myself feel better, I ate.

Once at a carnival, while I was stuck at the top of a Ferris wheel, I had what I thought was a great idea. I saw one of those booths below, where you stick your head through a hole, have your picture taken, and come out looking like either a weight lifter or Annie Oakley, and thought if I were to cut my head out of a photograph and tape it to the picture of someone else's gorgeous body, I would get a good idea of what I might look like if I were thin. So I did it. Unfortunately, the resulting creature just looked an awful lot like my head taped to someone else's gorgeous body.

I once had a friend suggest that we go on a diet together. The plan was this: We would each buy a padlock for our refrigerators, then trade padlocks, but retain the combination to the one we had purchased. This way, only I would know the combination to her padlock, and she, mine. On the surface, this sounded like a viable solution to our mutual problem of overeating. We gave up the idea, however, when we found ourselves planning an excessive number of overnights.

I have a good friend who recently got a divorce and, after successfully quitting for years, took up smoking cigarettes again in order to lose weight so she could get out there and compete in the dating scene. For a second, I actually wondered if I should start again. After all, at least twenty of these excess pounds suddenly appeared after I quit. But with the unquestionable reality of cigarettes causing cancer, thankfully, I just couldn't bring myself to light up again. Maybe I could just sneak outside when no one is looking and get a tan. Everyone knows that a tan'll make you look thinner, right? But then of course there's that little thing about skin cancer.

Have you ever experienced that sticky situation where you go into a Burger King and suddenly become self-conscious about what you are planning to order for yourself? I've found a way to minimize that embarrassment. I stride boldly up to the counter, order my usual two double Whoppers with cheese, two large fries, and (and here's the trick) *two* large cokes instead of one. The cokes make it appear to the untrained eye that my to-go order is for two people, not just me.

A friend of mine has a couple of variations on this same theme that she shared with me. When she gets to the counter, she either snaps her fingers dramatically in the air and says aloud, "Now, what did he say he wanted?" or she pulls a blank piece of paper from her purse and pretends to read her order from a prepared list.

All of this subterfuge probably doesn't really fool anyone, but it somehow helps to ease the immediate suffering and definitely contributes to the survival of the fattest.

*****

Don't you just hate shopping for clothes? I do. Who are they trying to kid calling the clothes that fit so many of us *half-sizes?* Half of a what? Half of a cow? And, if *that's* a half, just what would a *whole* look like? At least the people who call them ample, queen size, or better yet, extra large, begin to speak the truth.

I'm still trying to devise a way to overcome the shopping for new clothes blues. That's when everything you like is only available in size one, and everything you hate is in your size. It's having to tell the saleslady it wasn't what you were looking for after all. It's that stubborn zipper that insists you buy the next size larger. It's having to come up with a believable excuse when your significant other picks out some minuscule garment that just happened to catch his eye and waits expectantly for you to come out and model it for him. It's when the sales associate automatically directs you to the maternity department. It's trying to get far enough away from the mirrors in those tiny dressing rooms to give the illusion of smallness. After one of these shopping ordeals, I generally check in at the magazine racks to find the newest diet or gimmick offering the greatest results in the least amount of time. I must admit, it's a bit like chasing windmills. Just call me Doña Quickfixie, Woman of La Muncha . . .

One of the more recent war-on-fat weapons I've stumbled upon in my never-ending quest is the relatively new product called olestra. Olestra is made from "natural farm-grown soybeans" and is touted as having the ability to make potato chips and other snack foods taste just like the real thing, but with half the calories and none of the fat. There is, however (manufacturers admit in the very small print), only one minor drawback. For some people, olestra is said to go directly through the body, and oh, by the way, just happens to carry some important nutrients along with it.

When I first saw the olestra products proudly displayed on the shelves of my favorite grocery store, I have to admit that secretly I was a bit excited. I had friends who said the products were good, and they never had any nasty side effects. Truth is only a few people had those, and surely not anyone with a cast-iron stomach like mine! Even so, I did take five or ten seconds to wonder, am I so desperate that a fistful of potato chips is worth the risk of possibly becoming a nutritionally deprived person with an uncontrollable anal discharge? Then, glancing around to see if anyone was watching, I tossed a couple bags of chips onto the bottom rack of my grocery cart.

When I got home, it didn't take me long to tear into a bag of these wonder chips. In fact, I opened one just for the sustenance I thought would be necessary to put the rest of the groceries away. And you know what? THOSE CHIPS WERE REALLY GOOD! They DID taste like the real thing. In fact, they were so good, I found myself checking the label to make sure I'd picked up the product with the olestra in it. "Wow!" I thought to myself. "What a great find!" And so I ate more, because, after all, they do have only half the calories and none of the fat!

The next day, while I was waiting for our piano to be delivered, I was surprised by an ever-so-slight, shall we say drizzling, in the nethermost regions of my size something-X pink shorts. And a few minutes later, as I tossed the shorts into the washing machine, I wondered if perhaps the manufacturer would consider changing the product's name to OOPS!

The third definition of *survive* in *Merriam Webster's Collegiate Dictionary,* Tenth Edition, is "to continue to function or prosper despite; withstand." If there is one thing to be said on the positive side for those of us who really carry our weight, it is that we truly do withstand. We withstand the "compliments," the humiliations, the short-lived and ever-changing gimmicks, the myriad blatant and subliminal food indicators, the commercials, the lies, the messy shorts, the inevitable failures. Truth is, we even continue to function in spite of ourselves. We endure. We know that the nice thing about dieting is if one doesn't work, we just need to wait a few minutes for a new and better one to appear. Or we jump on a new bandwagon and surrender to cellulite. We go on to the next thing and, happily, through it all, we have not yet learned the meaning of the phrase "I give up."

May 1, 1998*—My oldest came home today and told me that in today's jargon "phat" (pronounced "fat") means cool. I've been waiting to hear that phrase spoken all my life. "Phat is cool." "Phat is cool." Has a real nice ring to it, don't you think?*

* * * * *

EPILARD

You Know You're Fat When...

- You detest words like *heavy, large, stocky,* and *jolly* and suspect that whenever you overhear them being used, it's in reference to you.
- You think that the women most men like to look at are far too skinny.
- You're convinced that mirrors in clothing stores make you look bigger than you actually are.
- You use the excuse that the dry cleaners shrunk your pantsuit.
- You're on the highway, following a truck whose bumper is emblazoned with a sign that says, "Extra Wide Load," and all you can think of is your butt.
- According to your insurance company's height/weight chart, you should be way taller than you are.
- You stand on the bathroom scale and lean first one direction, then another, until you find one that gives the illusion that you've lost at least a little weight.
- Before stepping onto the scale, you pee, poop, shave your legs, shave under your arms, clean

the wax out of your ears, pluck your eyebrows, blow your nose, remove the lint from your belly button, and pop your blackheads just to ensure you get an accurate reading.

- You won't stand naked in front of a mirror, and you're shocked when it happens by mistake.
- Presents alternate between a range of "X" sizes for your added comfort and boxes of chocolate candy.
- You catch yourself rationalizing, "Those 'string beans' will never make it through the famine."
- The clothes on the rack in your size are either printed with large, multicolored flowers or are solid black.
- You're sure you can't lose weight because historically all of the women in your family have been fat, except Aunt Molly, but she was weird, or adopted, or alien, or something . . .
- People think of your overcoat as a second skin.
- You lie about your weight on your driver's license.
- Even though you've lied about your weight on your driver's license, you'd still be embarrassed for anyone to read the false weight that was printed there. (There is, after all, a limit to the number of pounds you can whittle off the true number before the pimply young clerk

typing in your vital statistics is forced to groan, "Oh, *as i-uff.")*

- You hurry to walk next to someone fatter than you.
- Conversations with acquaintances you haven't seen for a while invariably begin with the comment, "You've lost weight, haven't you?"
- Your friends are fat. After all, you have so much in common: food, fat, discussing diets, cutting down skinny people.
- You have dimples when you're not smiling.
- Unbidden, the clerk at the clothing store gives you the "skinny" on which styles and colors are slenderizing.
- You gaze wistfully at the "before" pictures in diet ads.
- You're painfully aware that the acronym for "Fat is Beautiful" is FIB.
- One size doesn't fit all.
- The size of your clothes resembles an algebraic equation in that it is always some function of X.
- You find that you've become one with the motto "a waist is a terrible thing to mind."
- The airlines insist you pay for two tickets.
- You thought the hippie movement referred to a chubette doing the macarena.

- You still think heavy hands are overweight migrant workers.
- A stranger asks when you're going to have that baby; problem is, you're not pregnant.
- You believe that Aphrodite (a-fra-'dee-tee), the well-known Greek goddess of love, had a sister named Cellulite (sell-yü-'leet-ee), who was the lesser-known Greek goddess of fat.
- Your body continues to jog after you've stopped.

* * * * *

AFTERWORD

"A Matter of Dimensions"

The birds chattered loudly, impatient for the sun to appear against the lingering gray dawn. At their insistence, Bridey McKinney threw back her covers and sat up, dangling her chubby legs over the side of her bed. She looked across the room at the mirror on the closet door. A shadow-reflection of herself slowly emerged there and took on added definition with the onset of the early morning light. Bridey stood up, squinted, and slinked toward the glass, trying to perfect a look of seduction. She observed her image, blurred now by the lashes of her half-closed eyelids. The lashes softened the illusion; obscured a hulking reality into a vision of almost haunting beauty. The shadows lent gauntness to the otherwise meaty cheeks and hinted at a nonexistent waistline.

The voice of a disc jockey brayed as her radio alarm exploded into the 6:00 a.m. silence. As she spun around to turn off the alarm, out of the side of her eye, Bridey saw her nightgown clinging to her dimpled derriere. Lowering the volume on the blaring radio, she mumbled, "I think I'd rather be kept in the dark." She snatched her bathrobe from a hook on the back of the bedroom door, shoved her arms into the worn sleeves, and heatedly tied the belt at the waist. Leaving the bedroom, she couldn't resist one last backward glance at the mirror. The dimples, at least, had been successfully camouflaged.

Bridey flipped on the kitchen light, groaning at the congealed remnants of last night's binge. Swallowing back a rumbling queasiness, she filled one side of her sink with dishwater and scraped glop off the plates into the disposal side. Apprehensively, she padded into the living room. There, greasy popcorn bowls, half-empty beer mugs, and disposable tins of desiccating clam dip crowded the coffee and end tables. Bridey piled up the mess, took it to the kitchen, and dropped it into the dishwater with the rest.

Five minutes of radio news was segmented by two commercials: a bug spray advertisement proclaiming the end of termites and other household pests, and one for a new, time-released diet capsule, guaranteed to conquer even the most diehard of closet eaters. Bridey stared vacantly into the dishwater, fantasizing. Closet eater . . . *the north side construction project has been struck again by a mysterious, as yet unidentified vandal, who seems to go for and completely destroy the closets, while leaving the remainder of the structures virtually unscathed . . .*

The news was followed by a three-second weather report: *"Sunny* and *hot* are the weather words for today!" Bridey glanced up at the red plastic kitchen clock. Last night's dishes were done, and she was hungry. She opened the refrigerator, activating the newly installed, automatic shame machine. "What?" it crackled, "you eating again, fatso? You glutton! You're disgusting—only a pig eats more often than you do!"

Bridey grabbed two eggs from the grooved rack and snapped the door shut. "So's ya motha!" she shouted at the closed refrigerator. She set a frying pan on the stove, turned back to the refrigerator for butter, "What? You eating again, fatso? You glutton! You're . . .", and slammed the door.

While her eggs fried, Bridey dropped two slices of wheat bread into the toaster. "Oh, shit, the jelly!" she said aloud, mustering ego strength against the mechanized verbal bludgeoning. ". . . disgusting—only a pig . . ." She read the label on the jar she now held in her hand. "Well," she sighed, "it's not my favorite, but mint apple will just have to do."

At the breakfast table, Bridey flipped on the switch of her automatic fork and waited for the green "go" light to appear. When it did, she took her first bite, synchronizing the gnashing of her teeth with the beeps emitted by the fork. The fork beeped on, and Bridey chewed on, until the food turned to liquid between her grinding molars. The fork's light turned red and Bridey swallowed, awaiting the next green light that would be her signal to take another bite. She reached across the table for the magazine that had come in yesterday's mail and turned to the diet of the month. She quickly scanned the article. Irritated at finding nothing really new, she hurled the magazine against the wall, mumbling through her cud, "Only the names have been changed to make fools of the ignorant."

A piece of paper, mobilized by the violent flap of magazine wings, fluttered from the table to the floor. It was the map her friend Steve had drawn to a secluded beach he had discovered. Seeing it, Bridey cringed. In last night's more carefree state of drunkenness, she had made a commitment to be stronger than her embarrassment and go to the beach today to get some sun. Steve had sworn no one, not even he, would be there. "Very few people even know about it, as far as I can tell," he'd said.

Bridey carried her dirty dishes to the sink and tore a sheet from the notepad that hung on the kitchen wall. She uncapped a ball-point and listed the items she'd need to take to the beach: blanket, tanning oil, thermos of lemonade, sandwiches, ankle-length beach robe, sunglasses, sun hat, magazine, overblouse, automatic fork . . .

*****

Bridey shifted her eight-year-old, battle worn Vega into low gear. The car rolled to a stop at the intersection, the tired exhaust system erupting like a Gatling gun. Bridey referred to the penciled map on the bucket seat beside her. "Turn right at dead end." She looked up the road to her right, and on the horizon towered the large painted boulder designated "large painted boulder" on the map. The looming natural landmark was emblazoned with a spectacle of mismatched black letters on a white enamel background. "Elaine's Northwoods Buffeteria—Serve Yourself 'n Save." Below the message, a red arrow pointed toward a fissure in the immense evergreen wall. The dirt road seemed to end abruptly at the opening.

Halfway up the incline, a second sign beckoned. Three slats of wood, each fashioned after a very flat, very large-mouthed bass, were chained one below the other, undulating in the humid morning breeze. As Bridey turned to read the sign, her upper right arm made a popping sound as it released its liquid grasp on the seat back. "Minnows, worms, chubs," Bridey read. "Cheap shot!" she snorted, depressing the accelerator.

As the road took her deep into the woods, Bridey slowed down, allowing her eyes to adjust to the darkness. Dry needles crunched beneath the slow-rolling tires, and the smell of damp pine penetrated her nose. Off to her right lurked the ravaged remains of Elaine's. The sign above the boarded entrance had captured the Hamms Beer bear in the act of landing the elusive and legendary "big one." Buckshot peppered the log wall, blemishing the black spray paint that had once boldly professed the true love of Nina and Cubby. Bridey looked past the broken windows, remembering with some sadness how a hauntingly similar establishment had once looked inside . . .

> *. . . A player piano whirred and hummed and cranked out old song after older song, while a six-point buck, through plastic eyes studied the situation from his vantage point above the stone fireplace. A fox hide was splayed headless on the wall. Beside it, a typewritten, three-by-five card told the story of its capture. On the walls hung a collage of grinning raccoon heads, prize-winning walleyes, and smoke-bronzed snapshots, their curling edges framing proud moments of the kill. A black bearskin, head in tact, white teeth snarling around a pink plastic tongue, lay on the gray stone hearth as though waiting for just the right time to startle someone . . .*

Bridey started as a single drop of sweat trickled down the middle of her back. Again, she picked up the map. Steve had drawn a narrow lane to the left, a distance representing twenty yards beyond Elaine's cabin. The note beside it read, "take it slow." Bridey remembered Steve's words of caution as he sketched this part of the map. ". . . because there are some well-hidden ruts you'll come up against. But once you master them, the rest is easy."

Bridey's right foot rode the brake, allowing the car to idle gingerly over the craggy road. She cringed as the muffler scraped a rock and the ashtray regurgitated cigarette butts, adding to the pile already beginning to form at her feet. Managing to maneuver the hill by quarter inches, Bridey stopped at the crest, awed by the scene that stretched before her. The trees formed an arbor, shading a narrow path that lead downward into a cove of what appeared to be untrammeled virgin sand. At the mouth of the cove, the lake was a liquid mirror, reflecting a flawless image of the lone cumulus cloud that hung in an otherwise powder blue sky.

As she climbed out of the car, a breeze found the moisture that soaked the back of her beach robe. She rubbed the goosebumps on her arms as she walked around the car to the back. She unlocked the trunk and carefully lifted out her blue-speckled Styrofoam cooler. The wire grips were broken, making it necessary to carry the box in her arms. Balancing the cooler on her left hip, Bridey lifted a straw bag that was brimming with beachfront paraphernalia from the trunk. She slung the handle of the bag over her shoulder and with her free hand, shut the trunk lid.

Walking the path toward the beach, Bridey stumbled over an exposed, convoluted tree root, as a low-hanging branch clawed at the red bandanna that covered her head. Gaining her balance, she looked ahead and stopped short. There on the beach to her right, hidden from carside view, was a man lying quietly on his back.

"Damn! It's supposed to be deserted!" Bridey sputtered. Without a second thought, she pivoted to head back toward her car. As she did, the sun reflected off of the dark glasses the man was wearing, and Bridey turned back around to take a closer look. A German Shepherd lounged at the man's feet. The dog held his head proudly as he looked out over the water, his baloney tongue dangling lazily out the side of his mouth. What looked like the curved white handle of a cane stuck out from under one corner of the man's beach blanket.

"He's blind," thought Bridey, silently apologizing to God for the enormous relief she found in that fact.

The strap of the straw bag slid down her shoulder, and Bridey twisted to readjust it, brushing against a bush in the process. The dog's ears twitched and he cocked his head in her direction and barked. The man's head turned toward the sound, and he sat up. "Hello!" he hollered. "Name's Quinn!"

Bridey called back hesitantly. "Oh, hello, I'm Bridey, I didn't mean to bother . . ."

"And ya didn't! he shouted. "Look here, Dog and I have been savin' this bit of beach for ya." He bent sideways, swooping his right arm dramatically.

Bridey slowly approached them, keeping one leery eye on the dog. "For me? But I only just decided to come here this morning."

Quinn smiled broadly, revealing uneven, alabaster teeth. "Yes, you decided and sure enough, you're here."

Bridey piled her supplies on the sand a safe distance from the two of them. Absently she tugged at the sides of her beach robe, making sure it wasn't clinging to the ledge formed by her hips. She glanced self-consciously at Quinn, who sat quietly petting his dog, and felt foolish. She pulled the blanket from her straw carryall and spread it out on the sand. "So you know Steve Hurst?"

Quinn shook his head. "'Fraid I haven't had the pleasure."

"Then how did you know I'd be here?"

"Didn't."

Bridey knelt on her blanket and started to unpack the rest of her belongings. "But you said you and your dog saved this beach . . .?"

"We got here, and there was more beach than we needed, see."

Bridey uncapped her suntan oil and rubbed it lavishly over her arms and face, lifting her sunglasses to grease her cheekbones as she spoke. "Yeah, and?"

Quinn thought for a moment before answering. "Okay, maybe I can explain it this way. When you're hungry for Ritz crackers, say, you open a tube, take out what you want, and save the rest, right?"

"Rest?" Bridey thought sardonically, then said, "Okay, but what do Ritz crackers have to do with this beach?"

Quinn held up a hand. "I'm gettin' there. Okay, say now somebody comes along and eats the crackers that you saved. Up 'til now, you've just been savin' crackers, and *only* now do you know just who you were savin' 'em for."

"Oh, I get what you mean," said Bridey, debating whether she should take off the robe. Staring suspiciously at Quinn's black glasses, she waved her hand in front of his face. The dog whined and yipped once, snuggling closer to his master. Bridey moved back cautiously. "What did you say your dog's name is?"

"Dog."

"I guess that should be easy enough to remember."

Quinn grinned. "It is. It's also quite self-righteous. I label him Dog, see, and he in turn does dog stuff, like barking and licking and chewing up things that don't belong to him, which all serve to make my label work, and I get to be right."

Bridey unhooked the first four buttons of her robe, surveying the expanse of the beach and as far into the forest as her twenty-twenty vision would allow. Satisfied that they were alone, she slipped the robe down over her shoulders, exposing her bikinied self from the waist up.

"Smells like coconut oil," said Quinn.

Bridey nodded. "That's what it is. It really helps speed a tan along." She stared thoughtfully at the shimmering lake. A loon disappeared head first, leaving behind a rippling liquid target. Watching it, Bridey's thoughts were transported to another lake; a lake of her childhood. "I've been using it over half my life, now." She spoke as if to the loon, which had surfaced close to the shore. He glided easily over the water, head darting from side to side as though dodging a swarm of deer flies. His cry was mournful. Bridey looked back at Quinn. "This guy I used to know used it."

"And I suppose he was your average dark Greek god?"

Feeling as though Quinn had just read her thoughts, Bridey flushed. "Italian," she corrected him.

Quinn went on as though she hadn't said a word. "And your annual insistence on getting brown in the summer is still making him right after all these years." He shook his head and smiled crookedly. "Seems he made quite a groove on an impressionable pubescent mind."

"And what's that supposed to mean?" Bridey asked defensively.

Quinn didn't acknowledge her question, but went on. "And with such an Irish name, what color is your hair, Bridey?"

Not understanding where all this was leading, she answered. "Red, why?"

"And your eyes, Bridey?"

"Green, but . . ."

"And his eyes and hair were jet black. Am I right, Bridey?"

Bridey nodded while Quinn continued. "And because he just happened to use coconut oil, you made *it* totally responsible for the deep richness of his God-given olive hide. And so you apply it to your very fair and freckled skin, and because you *believe* that it works, your skin becomes golden, despite a very real lack of necessary pigmentation."

Bridey saw the image of her greased face and shoulders reflected in his sunglasses. Inches below the reflection, his mouth enunciated. "You're a powerful woman, Bridey."

Bridey squirted more coconut oil into her hand and rubbed it on her neck. Quinn cocked his head. "Like me to get your back?"

Envisioning his hands smoothing oil into the crevices of her meaty back, Bridey found herself almost shouting. “No! I mean . . . I can get it, thanks.”

“The suggestion bothered you, why?”

Bridey’s eyes nervously flitted back and forth as though scanning a mental montage of excuses. Surprising herself, she blurted out the truth of the matter. “I’m fat.”

“That greasy stuff I cut off a T-bone is fat . . . surely you’re something else.”

Feeling uncomfortable, Bridey started to squirm and tried to change the subject. “What do you say we just forget it, okay?”

“Must really hurt to give yourself such a beating. Care to talk about it?”

Bridey’s throat tightened, and her eyes brimmed with tears. “It all started when I met Michael. I was twelve of all things, a baby.” She rolled her eyes remembering. “But, God, I thought he must surely have been sent from heaven.”

“Your dark Greek god?” interjected Quinn.

Nodding, Bridey said, “Italian.” She spoke as though reading from a shoddy soap opera script. “He noticed me. Gave me a silver fifty cent piece for a tip. Showed me his brand new, fontaine blue Pontiac under the glittering stars, at a resort, on a lake just like this one, in the north woods of Wisconsin.”

A loon called out, and Bridey watched Dog stand up and take a few hesitant steps toward the lake. He licked his muzzle and barked importantly, then lay back down next to Quinn.

Bridey continued in her reverie. "He said loons were the keepers of lost souls." She shook her head, embarrassed at how remembering made her feel. "He was so handsome. He looked magnificent, and I found out later I had a piece of Oscar Meyer Wiener stuck between my front teeth."

Quinn sighed almost wearily and stretched out on this back, clasping his hands over his stomach. "And of course that inexcusable faux pas made you see what an unworthy, despicable character you really were."

Bridey lifted herself up on her arm and scooted out of the robe. She rubbed oil between her palms, then smoothed it over her legs. "I knew that very second I'd never have him. He was too good for me." Recapping the bottle, she reached into the cooler and took out a plastic bread sack, restuffed with sandwiches. She pulled out two of them and touched one to Quinn's clasped fingers. "Here," she smiled smugly. "Seems I brought this sandwich for you."

Quinn's face beamed as he took the sandwich. "Yes, you certainly did."

Bridey unscrewed the red plastic cup from her thermos and filled it with lemonade. Quinn turned his head toward the splashing sound. "What's that?"

"Lemonade . . . we'll have to share the cup." Bridey handed it to Quinn and squinted toward the sky. The sun was almost directly above them now. She shifted her position in order to get the full benefit of the tanning rays and picked up her sandwich. She slid the wrapper down so that the bottom half of the sandwich was still protected from her oily fingers. Absently she bit off a corner. "That's when I started eating like I heard grocery stores had been given 'til sundown to get out of town."

"That's rich," Quinn snorted. Taking a gulp of lemonade, he sat up again and wrapped his arms around his knees. "This oughta be good."

Bridey sank her teeth into her sandwich. "He said he'd write, and he did. Though not nearly as often as me." She washed the food down with a sip of lemonade. "Well, a couple of times, anyway." She popped the last bit of bread into her mouth. "Two of my friends and I met him at the lake the next summer. It was all arranged. We'd all stay in the same cabin together. By then I was really fat, but I didn't think it mattered. I was prepared to make the ultimate 'sacrifice of love.'"

Quinn sighed heavily and lowered his forehead to his knees. "So he helped himself to a naive, young, adoring virgin. Then what?"

Bridey hesitated, then whispered, "He asked Jake if he'd like to switch partners."

Quinn stretched out on his side and rested his head on his hand, eyebrows arched with curiosity.

"Oh, we didn't," Bridey assured him. "He and Jake left together the next day. Katie and I stayed at the cabin the rest of the week." She tore the third sandwich in two and handed half to Quinn. She looked at the shriveled dollop of dried catsup on the crust in her hand and set the sandwich down. "When I got home, Jake played me the tape he'd made of their trip back."

Quinn's voice was tender. "The one where your Italian laughed at you for what you did?"

Bridey nodded. "That's right," she said slowly. "He said I was stupid." Bridey's eyes questioned Quinn. "How come you know that?"

Quinn shrugged. "Simple. You *had* to have him say it, Bridey. Him or someone, because for some reason, that's how you needed to feel. It's like I said, you're an extremely powerful woman. You must remember that."

Bridey flashed a wry smile. "Yeah, I get it. And so then I decided to get even fatter and not see colors for a year as the punishment I deserved for being so stupid."

"*Did* you, now?"

"Yes, and from that experience, I learned how deeply I was capable of loving and how very painful loving can be." Bridey began to bubble with excitement. "I must love and love must hurt, right? It all works out just perfectly when I'm fat, so I stay a fat, though loving person?"

"Such dramatic drivel! Where does it all come from?" Quinn chided, watching sympathetically as Bridey's shoulders slumped in humiliation. His hand rested on a piece of driftwood. Thoughtfully, he sat up facing the water and tossed the wood into the lake. Dog pranced lightly over the sand and dove into the water in hot pursuit. Under the water, his paws paddled rhythmically, navigating his body around and to the right of the floating stick. He gently clasped the wood between his teeth as if he thought he might hurt it and headed proudly toward the shore. Dropping his catch at Quinn's feet, Dog shook himself violently, showering them both, and stood at attention, alert and eager for the next toss.

Quinn cupped the dog's chin in his left hand and scratched his damp, furry chest with his right. "Don't you see it all begins with the label, Bridey?" Dog whined in anticipation. His wet tongue lapped Quinn's cheek, and his feet danced as though burned by the sand. Quinn hurled the stick out onto the water again, and Dog chased after it. Quinn turned to Bridey. "Dog will always do dog stuff, because he's powerless to change the label." He touched her hand with a sandy index finger. "But you, Bridey. You can go inside yourself and find out who you really are. Get past those things you've always said are you. And when you see it can be different, you must change the label."

Quinn stood up and grabbed his blanket by two corners. He snapped it free of sand and folded it neatly, securing it under his left arm. He bent over and grasped the ornate handle of his ivory walking stick.

A cool breeze whispered through the trees and shuffled the pages of the diet magazine at Bridey's side. Quinn touched the magazine with his staff, drawing Bridey's attention to the dog-eared article. "At Last! The Miracle Diet You've Been Waiting For!" he read aloud.

Bridey's eyes rolled carefully over the words Quinn had just read, crawled slowly up the length of the hand-carved walking stick, over his clenched hand, extended arm, and finally rested on his solemn face. She stood up facing him, her nose almost touching his, and found his eyes in lock with hers behind the dark lenses. She envisioned her earlier self deciding to approach the beach only because she thought he couldn't see her. "You're not blind," she whispered. "All this time I thought you . . ."

Quinn's smile was warm. "Never wait for someone else to give you freedom, when all you really have to do is choose it for yourself." He whistled for Dog, who bounded toward him, and together they turned and walked away from her and down the beach. As though frozen in that time and that space, Bridey stared after them. Quinn turned, and making a megaphone of his hands, hollered, "Just look at you standing so proudly in a bikini. And on a public beach at that!"

Bridey watched until they had disappeared from sight, then looked down at the array of equipment that cluttered her beach blanket and clearly saw her life. Dropping to her knees, she dug a hole in the sand deep enough to hold the ankle-length robe, the overblouse, the diet magazine, and the automatic fork. These she placed into the hole and covered with sand.

They were the things of a fat person. None of it really her stuff after all.

* * * * *

Appendix 1

Foodspeak

Holiday Word Associations

Cue	Response
New Year's Eve	Champagne
Valentine's Day	Candy
Washington's Birthday	Cherry Pie
St. Patrick's Day	Corned Beef 'n Cabbage/Green Beer
Easter	Eggs/Candy
Memorial Day	Picnic
Fourth of July	Picnic
Birthday	Cake
Wedding	Cake
Labor Day	Barbecue
Halloween	Candy
Thanksgiving	Turkey/Dinner
Christmas	Goose/Dinner/Candy/ Plum Pudding

Geographical Word Associations

Cue	Response
Alaska	Baked
California	Avocado
Florida	Orange Juice
Georgia	Peach
Idaho	Potatoes
Iowa	Corn/Pork Sandwich
Kansas	Wheat
Kentucky	Bourbon/Ham

Maine .... Lobster
Mississippi .... Mud Pie
New York .... Steak/Cheesecake
Ohio .... Buckeyes
Texas .... Toast
Vermont .... Maple/White Cheddar
Virginia .... Ham
Washington .... Apple
Wisconsin .... Cheese
Long Island .... Iced Tea
Altoona .... On Toast
Boston .... Baked Beans/Cream Pie
Buffalo .... Burger
Concord .... Grape
Denver .... Omelet/Sandwich
Frankfurt .... er
Kansas City .... Barbecue
London .... Broil
Philadelphia .... Cream Cheese/
Steak Sandwich
Sacramento .... Tomato Juice
Salisbury .... Steak
San Francisco .... Sour Dough

Edible Handles

Candy, Basil, Brie, Newton (apple), Carmel, Cherry, (filet) Mignon, Ginger, Sherry, Cookie, Filbert, Melba (toast), Margarita, Honey, Jonathan (apple), Colby (cheese), Brandy, Graham (cracker), (eggs) Benedict, Taffy, Stew, and Olive.

Succulent Surnames

Bacon, Bartlett (pear), Bass, Bean, Berry, Burger, Cane, Carne, Cherry, (corn) Cobb, Coco, Coffee, Colby (cheese), (ice cream) Cone, Cornish (hen), Crab, Dill (pickle), Fish, (sweet) Gerkin, Graham (cracker), Ham, Hershey (bar), Herring, Lamb, Lemons, Maple, Olive, Pepper, Plum, Rice, Roll, Romano, Sage, Salmon, Whiting, and Wiener!

Taste-Tantalizing Street Names

Cherry Lane, Berry Avenue, Burgundy Drive, Chestnut Drive, Elderberry Road, Fig Way, Filbert Court, Ginger Court, Grape Street, Hickory (nut) Place, Honey Way, Maple Avenue, Olive Street, Orange Court, Peach Way, Pheasant Run Parkway, Plum Place, Rice Circle, Turkey Creek Canyon Road, and Walnut Street.

People as the Basic Food Groups

Meat, Fish, and Fowl. A shrimp, a meathead, a muttonhead, a brain, a muscle, a lucky duck, a silly goose, a porker, a crab, a sucker, a shark, an octopus, a ham, a jellyfish, a chicken, a snail, a lamb, a meatball, and former Vice President Quayle.

Vegetables. String beans, a young sprout, a pea brain, tomatoes, two peas in a pod, unfortunates with cauliflower ears, cool cucumbers, carrottops, couch potatoes, corny folks, and former President Reagan.

Dairy Selections. The cream of the crop, an egghead, a butterball, a butterfingers, a good egg, a dip, and a big cheese.

Nuts and Fruits. A nut, a tough nut to crack, a peanut, a fruit, a peach, the apple of your eye, a bad apple, a hayseed, a bad seed, a seedy character, a kiwi, an old prune, or someone who's just gone bananas.

Carbohydrates. A Caspar Milquetoast, a crackerjack, a fruitcake, a tough little cookie, a cracker, a sweetie, a honey, a creme puff, a sucker, a jelly belly, a sugar daddy, a little tart, the upper crust, Mama's little dumpling, the toast of the town, or someone who is off her noodle.

Music

Oldies Groups. Hot Chocolate, Bread, Brown Sugar, Cream, Tuna, Meatloaf, Wild Cherry, Bing (cherry) Crosby, Chuck Berry, and the Platters.

Possible Oldies Call-in Requests. "Blueberry Hill," "Lemon Tree," "Tangerine," "On the Good Ship Lollipop," "I Like Peanut Butter" "American Pie," "Lady Marmalade," "The Days of Wine and Roses," "Strawberry Fields Forever," "Summer Wine," "Yes! We Have No Bananas," "Polk Salad Annie," "One Bourbon, One Scotch, and One Beer," "Tea for Two," "Octopus's (vegetable) Garden," "Wasted Away Again in Margaritaville," "Mean Mr. Mustard," "A Spoonful of Sugar Helps the Medicine Go Down," "I Heard It Through the Grapevine," "Popcorn," "Chopsticks," "The Beer

Barrel Polka," and, maybe just a little too close to home, "I'm Just a Junk Food Junkie."

Today's Performers. Blind Melon, Black Grape, The Cranberries, Fiona Apple, Lemonheads, Smashing Pumpkins, Salt, Sugar, Spice Girls, and Salt 'n Peppa.

Children's Television Shows

Samurai Pizza Cats, Bananas in Pajamas, Beetlejuice, Gummi Bears, Sesame Street, and *Lamb Chop's Play Along.*

Cooking Gurus

The Frugal Gourmet, The Galloping Gourmet, Baking with Julia, Great Chefs: Great Cities, Louisiana Cookin', Great Chefs of the South, Yan Can Cook, Emeril Live, and my personal favorite, *Two Fat Ladies.*

Movies

Meatballs, Honey I Shrunk the Kids (Blew up the Kid, Shrunk Ourselves), The Days of Wine and Roses, There's a Sucker Born Every Minute, Eating Raoul, Willie Wonka and the Chocolate Factory, Please Don't Eat the Daisies, The Three Musketeers, James and the Giant Peach, Canadian Bacon, and *Like Water for Chocolate.*

Celebrities

Kevin Bacon, John Candy, Jack Lemmon, Sean Bean, Joseph Bologna, Jeff Mustard, Carolyn Farina, Diane Baker, and Barbara Hershey.

Everyday Expressions

You are what you eat.
You can tell them anything you want, except, just don't spill the beans.
That story's really hard to swallow.
Eat your heart out.
Be careful, or you're gonna eat your words.
Don't worry, we all know what it feels like to eat crow.
In life it always helps to know exactly which side your bread is buttered on.
If I'm wrong, I'll find myself eating humble pie.
That young'n's really feeling his oats.
That little vixen finally got her just desserts.
I doubt if that know-nothing can cut the mustard.
The way to a man's heart is through his stomach.
She was born with a silver spoon in her mouth.
He was left standing there with egg on his face.
Man does not live by bread alone.
Bread is the staff of life.
That really takes the cake!
The surprise party was the icing on the cake.
This job is a piece of cake.
Old butter makes good cake.
The proof of the pudding is in the eating.
It's as American as apple pie.
An apple a day keeps the doctor away.
One bad apple spoils the whole barrel.
He was busier than a cranberry merchant at Christmas.
Too many cooks spoil the broth.
In a pickle.

In a jam.
In a stew.
She was sweet as honey.
He was slow as molasses on a winter day.
I'd like to live off the fat of the land.
That job's my bread and butter.
"She can bring home the bacon, fry it up in a pan."
His goose is cooked.
He'll never amount to a hill of beans.
That sounds like a fishy story to me.
I'll take that with a grain of salt.
If that guy even thinks about touching my sister, he's toast.

* * * * *

Appendix 2

Big Fat Lies

Personal Revelations

- I eat too much.
- I don't eat enough.
- I don't have fat, I have cellulose.
- I don't have fat or cellulose, I have adipose tissue.
- I was born with more fat cells than skinny people.
- I don't feel loved, so I turn to a surrogate: food.
- I got the fat gene.
- I contracted the fat virus.
- I was weaned too early.
- I have an oral fixation.
- I have a lower metabolism than skinny people.
- I have big bones.
- I like being fat.
- I can't deal with reality, so I hide from it behind this barrier of fat.
- I'm afraid to face life as a thin person.
- I have an allergy to carbohydrates; my body turns them into fat.
- I want people to feel sorry for me.
- I have no self-control.

- I am plotted against by friends and family who dare to serve anything but celery and carrot sticks.
- My parents never really wanted me and as punishment taught me bad food habits.
- I have an underactive thyroid.
- I am suicidal and have chosen a lingering as opposed to a quick death.
- I know it's wrong to enjoy sex, so I stay fat, because a fat girl hardly ever gets asked.
- I had a fat, significant someone in my childhood whom I am subconsciously trying to emulate.
- I want people to like me for what I am inside.
- I'm poor and can't afford anything but junk food.
- I'm addicted to chocolate.
- I was cruel to a fat person in one of my past lives, and my karma is finally catching up with me.

Weight-Loss Revelations

- Grapefruit causes fat to melt off your body.
- Grapefruit has no mysterious qualities.
- Fats are bad for you.
- Fats are necessary to sustain life.
- Exercise doesn't do any good.
- Exercise is crucial.

- If you eat only protein and no carbohydrates, you'll lose weight.
- If you eat only protein and no carbohydrates, you'll destroy your kidneys.
- If you eat only carbohydrates and no protein, you'll lose weight.
- If you eat only carbohydrates and no protein, you'll gain weight.
- Fasting is healthy.
- Fasting breaks down valuable muscle tissue.
- Fasting lowers an already too-low metabolism.
- You should always supplement your diet with vitamins.
- If you eat right, you won't need vitamins.
- When you reach a plateau, cut your calories in half to begin losing again.
- When you reach a plateau, "shock" your body with large ingestions of carbohydrates to begin losing again.
- Calories don't count.
- Calories do count.
- The only way to lose weight is to cut out certain prohibited foods.
- The only way to lose weight is to cut down, not out.
- You should eat what you want, when you want it.
- You must only eat at certain times of the day and choose foods from a narrowly defined list.

- Fat people have no willpower.
- Fat people have plenty of willpower, just no won't power.
- You should eat three meals a day.
- You should eat six small meals a day.
- You should never eat anything after 6:00 p.m.
- You should "graze" on food throughout the day.
- It doesn't make any difference what time you consume your calories.
- You should exercise in the morning.
- It's best to exercise after your dinner meal.
- Exercise increases a person's appetite.
- Exercise takes away the urge to eat.
- You can eat all the nonfat foods you want.
- You should limit your intake of nonfat foods.
- You should weigh yourself once a day.
- You should only weigh yourself once a week.
- You should throw away your bathroom scale.

* * * * *

Appendix 3

A Select Sampling of Survival Support Systems

Realizing that a *"little fat book"* might be somewhat of an oxymoron, my publisher asked if I would consider plumping it up just a bit by adding a section on support systems. It sounded like a good idea to me, because, after all, the various support systems one way or another do help in the ultimate survival of the fattest.

Given the assignment, my initial plan was to do a bit of research to find out what was "out there" and create a little list for insertion here. But what I came upon in my search was an array of information far too grand to squeeze into a little list at the back of a little book. Because there is so much information available and, more importantly, because I would not feel comfortable endorsing organizations I know nothing about, I decided instead to provide information here about some of the sources I have either had firsthand (or through close friends, first-and-a-half-hand) experience with, and to supplement it by saying that there is a huge support network waiting for you, whether your current mode of survival involves quick weight loss, slow and sensible weight loss, herbal weight loss, drug therapy weight loss, hypnotic weight loss, online personalized interactive weight loss, surgical weight loss, the latest weight-loss fads, exercise routines, exercise equipment, group fat chats in person or fat chatting on-line in the comfort of your own home, reading about weight loss, or even celebrating the

---

Publisher's Note: The names, physical addresses, tel/fax numbers, web site addresses and E-mail addresses provided in this appendix were verified prior to publication of this work, but are subject to change or cancellation at any time.

fact that you are fat with a growing contingency of like-minded folk. If you have access to the Internet, I promise that you will be overwhelmed by the number of matches you will hit by just entering the keywords: *weight loss, exercise programs,* or *fat acceptance.*

INTERNET SOURCES

Richard Simmons's Never Give up Club (http://www.richardsimmons.com)

This site offers daily, upbeat inspirational messages from Richard, success stories, recipes, exercise advice, and information about exercise videos, weight-loss programs, and Carnival "Cruise to Lose" vacations. You can join Richard's Clubhouse and have available a 24-hour, 7-day-a-week chatroom where you can talk to other people who are dealing with weight-loss challenges. Richard has a personals section where, if you'd like, you could meet a weight-loss or exercise buddy.

Rosie O'Donnel's Chub Club (http://rosieo.warnerbros.com)

Rosie's Chub Club does not recommend a specific diet plan; instead, it encourages members simply to commit to eating less and moving more. The site offers information about upcoming 5K walk/run events, healthy and inspirational tips, information about how you and three other people can start your own Chub Club for group support, and a weekly Rosies' Chub Club Calendar to help you monitor your own personal successes.

MAGAZINES/NEWSLETTERS

Fat!So?

A magazine for people who don't apologize for their size. The magazine shies away from fat-hate articles and instead focuses on pieces that attempt to break the taboos that surround being fat. It encourages articles from people who want to express their feelings (rage, dismay, delight) about comments, attitudes, or incidents they have experienced when body size was the issue. Other articles talk about lessons people have learned from being fat or how people derive joy from their body's size.

Contact: marilyn@fatso.com.

Prevention

A monthly magazine whose focus is fitness and healthy living. It contains articles that are at the forefront of the latest medical, nutritional, herbal, fitness, weight-loss news. Each issue offers information about Prevention's Walking Club, inspirational stories about people who have overcome their health/weight problems, shares healthy recipes; and talks about ways to maintain your health, your aging parents' health, your children's health, and even your pets' health.

Contact: Prevention Customer Service
P.O. Box 7319, Red Oak, IA 51591
Tel: (800) 813-8070
Web: http://www.healthyideas.com.

Radiance

A quarterly magazine that "celebrates women of all sizes of large, of all ages, lifestyles, and ethnicities." Each issue provides profiles of successful, dynamic, large women from all walks of life. Through articles on health, media, fashion, and politics, the magazine encourages readers to live healthy, full, active lives no matter what their size, and always with a heavy dose of self-love and self-esteem. At least once a year the magazine prints essays written by kids of all ages about their lives, bodies, struggles, and successes. The magazine also provides helpful information on how to help kids feel acknowledged, loved, and valued, no matter what size or shape they happen to be. *Radiance* is considered one of the leading sources of support, information, and inspiration to women in the worldwide Size Acceptance Movement.

Contact: Radiance
P.O. Box 30246, Oakland, CA 94604
Tel: (510) 482-0680
E-mail: Radmag2@aol.com
Web: http://www.radiancemagazine.com

Richard Simmons & Friends

A newsletter filled with motivational and inspirational tips for exercise and weight loss that are designed to help you make positive lifestyle changes that will help you reach and maintain your healthy weight. The newsletter is published ten times a year. Each issue features a personal message from Richard, the latest information on nutrition and exercise, a personal weight-loss success story dubbed the Cinderella Story, new healthy recipes, and more.

Contact: Threshold Publishing, LLC
1750 Old Meadow Rd, Third Floor,
McLean, VA 22102.

Weight Watchers Magazine

This magazine is bursting with articles on all aspects of weight loss management, including news about health, fitness, nutrition, and beauty. It is printed nine times a year, offers advice on how to stay in control of your healthy program whether you're at home, at a party, at a business lunch, or on a vacation. It offers seasonal recipes and fashion tips for concealing or otherwise dealing with a larger-than-average body. And for further motivation, each issue offers profiles of several people who have succeeded in reaching their weight-loss goals.

Contact: Weight Watchers Magazine
Box 56129, Boulder, CO 80322.
Tel: (800) 876-8441

WEIGHT ACCEPTANCE SOURCES

International Alliance for Size Acceptance (IASA)

IASA is an international alliance of many independent small acceptance groups and organizations, whose purpose is to build cohesion and implement vital communications among size advocates and activists. "The Alliance extends an open invitation to the individuals who would like to bring the fight for size acceptance to their country and act as an ambassador for this cause, a contact person, an ally perhaps for others to rally around." There is no cost to join the Alliance.

Contact: *Web:* http://www.size-acceptance.org.

Largesse, the Network for Size Esteem

Largesse is an "international clearinghouse for information on size diversity empowerment," who, since 1986, have helped "link individuals, groups, businesses, and professionals in the size rights community with information, support, and each other."

Their goal is to encourage awareness and social change that promote a positive image, health, and equal rights for people of size.

Contact: *E-mail:* largesse@eskimo.com.

National Association to Advance Fat Acceptance (NAAFA)

NAAFA is a nonprofit human rights organization whose mission since 1969 has been to improve the quality of life for fat people. NAAFA works to rid the world of discrimination based on body size and to provide people of size with necessary tools for self-empowerment via public education, member support, and advocacy.
Contact: *Web:* http://www.naafa.org.

WEIGHT-LOSS ORGANIZATIONS

First Place

Since 1981, First Place, an international Christ-centered program, has provided health and weight-management support to small groups (up to 20 people) meeting in churches of all denominations. First Place offers a 13-week program that uses a support system incorporating Bible study, prayer, behavior modification, exercise, and a healthy food plan to influence lifelong, healthy lifestyle changes and "helps participants focus on giving Christ 'First Place' in every area of their lives." The "Live It" food plan coincides with what is medically recommended for healthy living and is similar to the diabetic exchange program. Meetings are centered around food planning, group sharing, Bible Study, and prayer. Joining members are asked to purchase one of seven Bible studies and a member manual that includes, among other things, fact sheets, recipes, and the "Live It" food program.

Contact: *Tel:* (800) 727-5223
Web: http://www.firstplace.org

OPTIFAST

OPTIFAST is a therapy designed to help medically at-risk obese patients (people who have a body mass index or BMI greater than 30, or people who are 130% of their ideal body weight) improve their health and lower weight-related health risks like high cholesterol, hypertension, diabetes, and sleep apnea. The program involves consumption of OPTIFAST Formula, which provides 100% of the recommended daily requirements for vitamins and minerals, or nutritional bars that provide 25% or more of daily requirements. OPTIFAST is provided by physicians trained in obesity management, and patients are regularly monitored by registered dieticians. Medical monitoring includes frequent blood chemistry analysis and EKGs. Health professionals provide counsel in the areas of lifestyle modification, exercise, and nutrition. You can opt to receive such counseling individually or as a member of a group.

Contact: *Tel:* (800) 662-2540
Web: http://www.optifast.com

Overeaters Anonymous (OA)

OA is an international nonprofit organization that has been in existence since 1960, providing volunteer support groups for people from all walks of life who meet in order to help solve their mutual problem of compulsive overeating. OA is patterned after the Twelve-Step Alcoholics Anonymous program and addresses physical, emotional, and spiritual recovery aspects of compulsive overeating. OA does not recommend a specific diet plan; instead, they encourage members to use an eating/exercise plan provided by health professionals. OA does not claim to be a diet club and makes no claims regarding weight loss. Their fundamental concept is that if members acknowledge their past inability to control compulsive overeating and abandon the idea that a little willpower is all that they need to be able to eat normally, it will become possible for them to stop overeating—one day at a time. There are no membership dues or fees, although most groups request voluntary donations at meetings to cover expenses.

Contact: Overeaters Anonymous
P.O Box 44020
Rio Rancho, NM 87124-4020
Tel: (505) 891-2664
E-mail: overeatr@technet.nm.org

TOPS (Take off Pounds Sensibly)

TOPS is a nonprofit, noncommercial, worldwide organization that was founded in 1948 and provides the support, encouragement, and education needed to make healthy, permanent, lifestyle changes using an eating/exercise plan provided by your doctor. TOPS meetings are held weekly and are lead by volunteer members and sometimes supplemented by input from physicians, nutritionists, psychologists, or other experts who volunteer their time to speak. In addition to meetings, confidential weigh-ins, and the support and encouragement of other members, TOPS offers a monthly magazine and information on motivational workshops, rallies, and retreats. To join you are asked to pay a small annual membership fee, and dues are set by local chapters to cover minimal expenses.

Contact: *Tel:* (800) 932-8677
Web: http://www.tops.org

Weight Watchers

Weight Watchers is a worldwide organization that for more than three decades has helped people achieve their weight-management goals in a safe and supportive group environment. Weight Watchers provides an education program that stresses a comprehensive approach to weight management that is built on the latest scientific principles in the areas of nutrition, behavior, and exercise and is designed to achieve positive lifestyle changes. The program consists of a food plan that meets nutritional recommendations of major health organizations and is designed to promote a healthful rate of weight loss, an activity plan that emphasizes toning, stretching, and calorie-burning activities, and a behavioral support plan that focuses on your individual needs. For member convenience, Weight Watchers offers meetings at various times and places and even offers at-work programs if there is sufficient interest. The meetings begin with a confidential weigh-in and are lead by people who have already lost and maintained their weight on the Weight Watchers program. Leaders have undergone training to ensure their understanding of the Weight Watchers program. In addition to group sharing and support, at meetings you can get the latest information about nutrition, physical activity, and behavior modification. To join, you are asked to pay a registration fee (sometimes these are waived during special promotions) in addition to a weekly fee.

For those who either don't have the time or are not comfortable attending group meetings, Weight Watchers has developed an at-home program through which you can get all the program basics, the latest nutrition and exercise information, and phone support when you need it. For this program, you are asked to pay a one-time charge.

Contact: *Tel:* (800) 651-6000
Web: http://www.weightwatchers.com

* * * * *

ABOUT THE AUTHOR

Linda Frantzen Carlson works as a freelance editor and proofreader and lives in Colorado with her husband, Randy, and daughters, Tessa and Traci.

She has written play reviews, feature articles, satire, greeting cards, and poetry for various publications since 1982 and for more than eight years was a Boulder Colorado newspaper columnist.

*PLUMP: **survival of the fattest*** is her first book-length work.

ABOUT WHITE-BOUCKE PUBLISHING

White-Boucke publishes general nonfiction books (many of a humorous nature) and specialized reference books. For a free copy of our catalog, contact:

WHITE-BOUCKE PUBLISHING, INC.
PO BOX 400, LAFAYETTE, CO 80026, USA
tel: (303) 604-0661, fax: (303) 604-0662
e-mail: ordering@white-boucke.com

Our full range of books, CDs/audiotapes, videotapes and details of special services can also be found on our Internet World Wide Web site:

http://www.white-boucke.com